SEA LION RESEARCH
3 - MAY 200
(PORT PEGASUS)
BLUFF - STEWART ISLAND - AUCKLAND ISLANDS -
STEWART ISLAND (PORT WILLIAMS) - BLUFF
ON BOARD THE VESSEL
BREAKSEA GIRL

New Zealand's
SUBANTARCTIC ISLANDS

SKIPPER
Lance Shaw
Lance Shaw

CREW

Ruth Dalley
Ruth Dalley

Essie Steven
E Steven

Erik Ashton
E Ashton

John Lawes

[signature]

DIVERS FOR MUSEUM OF
NEW ZEALAND TE PAPA TONGAREWA
BOB SHAW
ERIK ASHTON

RESEARCH TEAM
IAN WILKINSON
[signature]

Simon Childerhouse
S Childerhouse

Nadine Gibbs
[signature]

[signature] GARETH JONES

PADRAIG J. DUIGNAN
Padraig Duignan

ASSISTANTS
Hera Sengers
[signature]

Taco Viel's
P Viel's

New Zealand's Subantarctic Islands

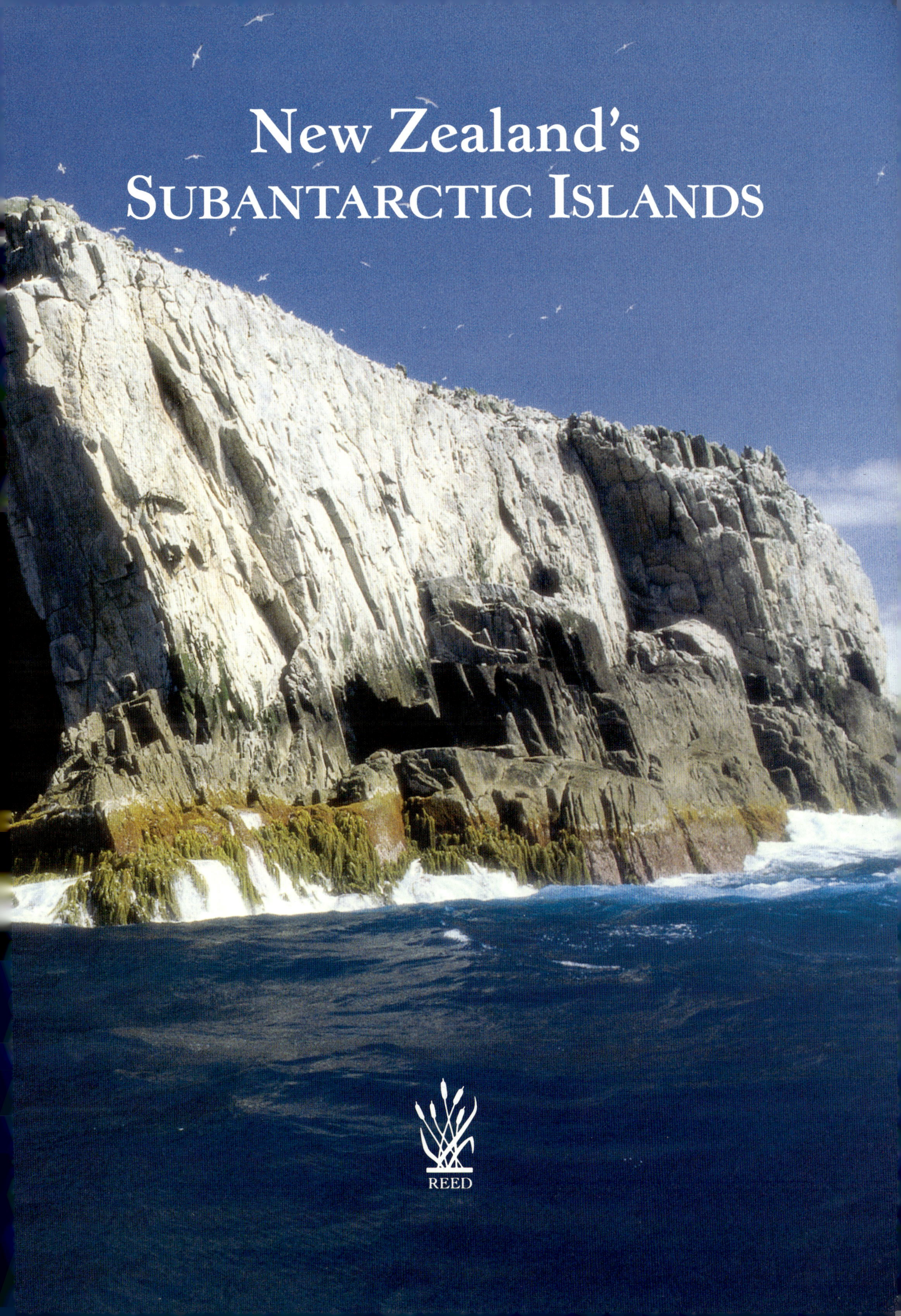

Front cover photographs:
Adams Island (Craig Potton); New Zealand (Hooker's) sea lion, female pup (Lou Sanson); *Bulbinella rossii* and *Anisotome latifolia*, Enderby Island, Auckland Islands (Chris Rance); Erect-crested penguins (Andrea Booth); Salvin's mollymawk and chick (Andrea Booth).

Back cover photographs:
Koaro (G.A. Eldon); seaweeds at Snares Islands (Carol West); *Insulanoplectron spinosum*, Snares Islands (Mike Meads).

Title page:
Funnel Island, Bounty Islands (Andrea Booth).

Contents page:
Pleurophyllum speciosum, Campbell Island (Carol West).

Published by Reed Books, a division of Reed Publishing (NZ) Ltd, 39 Rawene Rd, Birkenhead, Auckland. Associated companies, branches and representatives throughout the world. Website: www.reed.co.nz

This book is copyright. Except for the purpose of fair reviewing, no part of this publication may be reproduced or transmitted in any form or by any means, electronic or mechanical, including photocopying, recording, or any information storage and retrieval system, without permission in writing from the publisher. Infringers of copyright render themselves liable to prosecution.

© 1999 Crown Copyright
Photographs property of photographers/DoC

ISBN 0 7900 0719 3
First published 1999

Printed in New Zealand

Dedication

Dedicated to the memory of Gerry Clark and Roger Sales, who perished when their yacht *Totorore* was wrecked off the southern coast of Antipodes Island in June 1999.

Acknowledgements

This book is a revised and updated edition of *New Zealand's Subantarctic Islands: A Guidebook*, edited by Tim Higham and published in 1991. Some chapters required little if any amendment; others, like the chapter on freshwater fauna, required a substantial amount of work to cover recent research. Individual chapters have been reviewed and amended where appropriate by the following:

The International Setting — Lou Sanson; History — Rachael Egerton; Geology — Ian Turnbull; Soils — Alan Hewitt; Vegetation — Carol West and Brian Rance; Invertebrates — John Marris; Birds — Pete McClelland; Freshwater Fauna — Lindsay Chadderton, Mike Winterbourn and Mike Joy; Seals and Whales — Simon Childerhouse; Marine Life — Wendy Nelson and Chris Battershill; Introduced Species — Andy Cox and Carol West; Key Visitor Sites — Greg Lind; Code of Conduct — Greg Lind.

A special thanks to Mark Day for picture selection and map production and Dr Carol West for editing scientific amendments and to the Royal New Zealand Navy, Rodney Russ and Super Nova Expeditions Ltd, without whose support, often in difficult conditions, much of the important work carried out on the islands would be impossible.

Tom O'Connor
Senior Editor
Department of Conservation, 1999

CONTENTS

Introduction	9
The International Setting	13
History	17
Geology	25
Soils	35
Climate	37
Vegetation	42
Invertebrates	54
Birds	58
Freshwater Fauna	73
Seals and Whales	77
Marine Life	86
Introduced Species	90
Key Visitor Sites	93
Code of Conduct	100
Further Reading	102

8 New Zealand's Subantarctic Islands

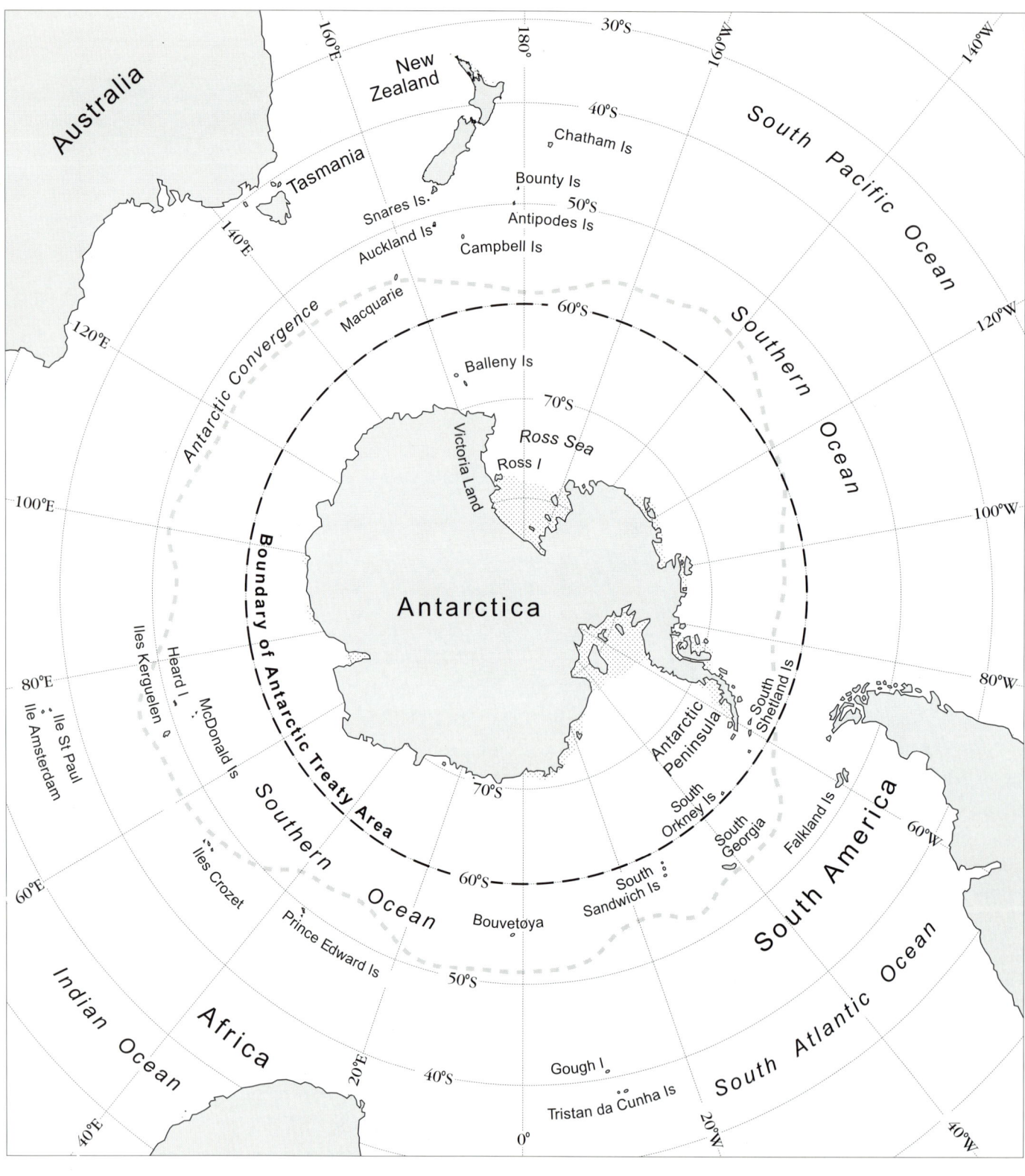

Introduction

New Zealand's five subantarctic island groups are among the most isolated of the country's territories. As National Nature Reserves and New Zealand's third World Heritage Area, they are as unique as our national parks and as important as the most outstanding natural conservation areas in the world.

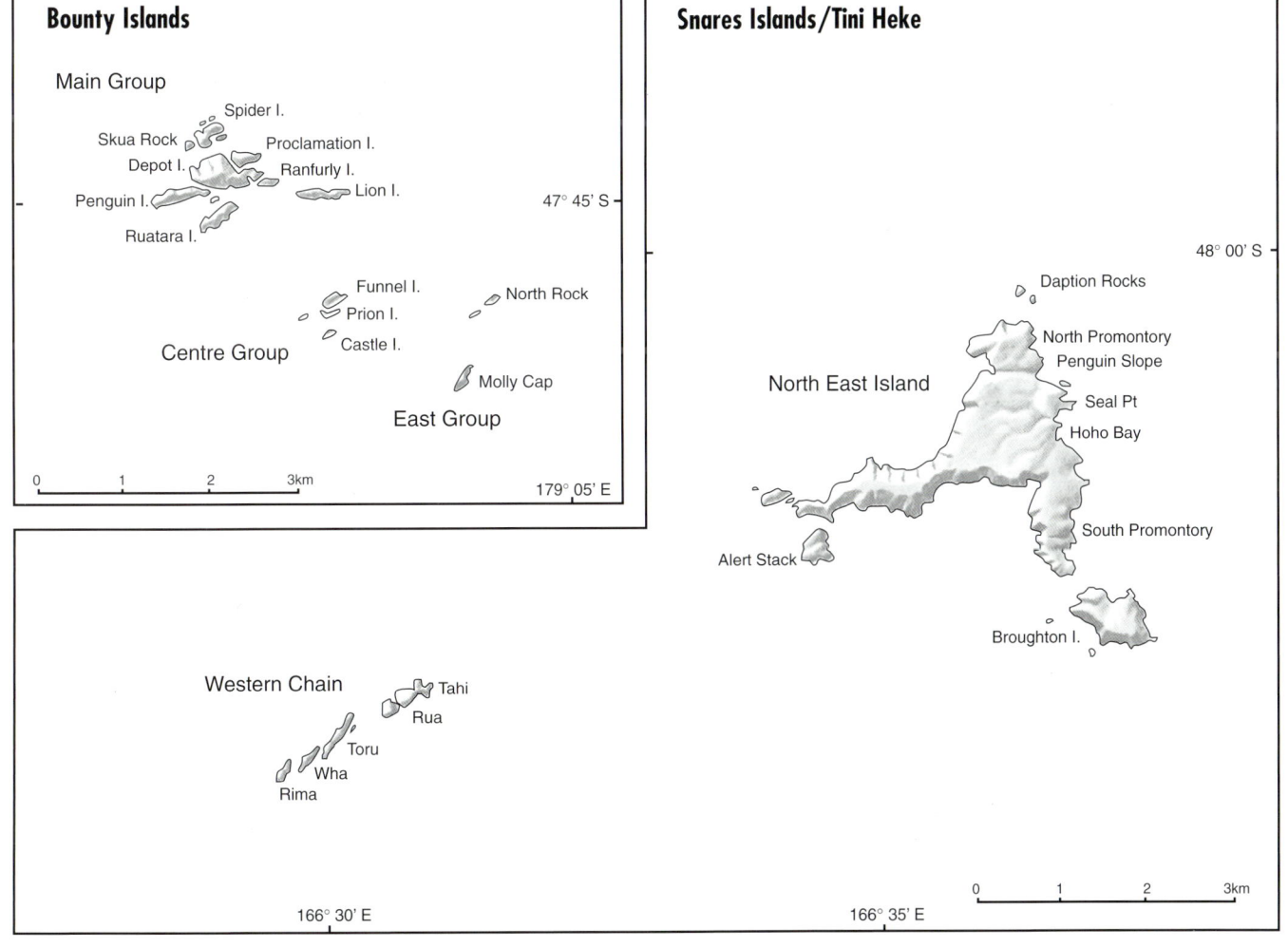

10 New Zealand's Subantarctic Islands

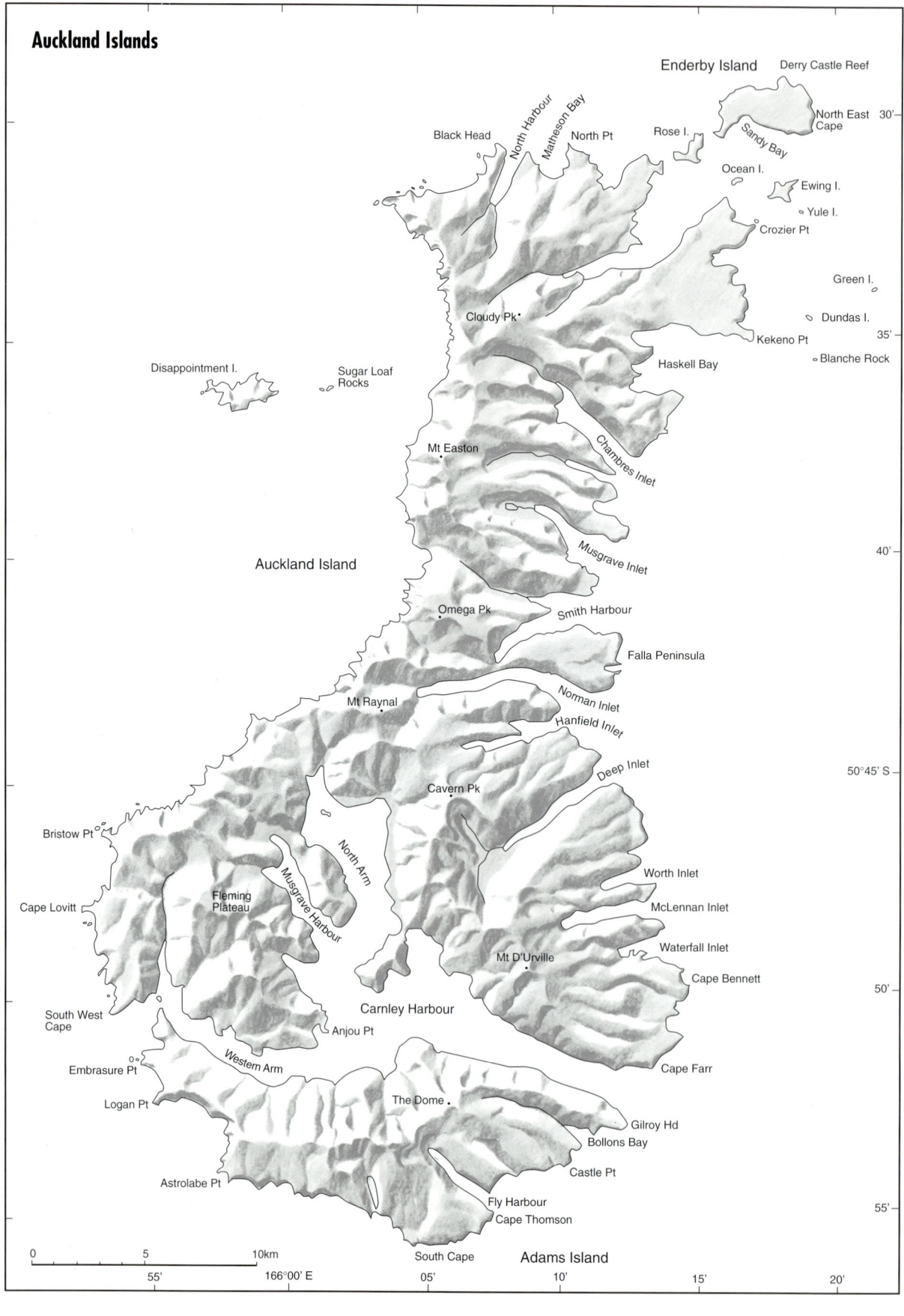

Introduction

The five island groups and the ocean around them are one of the last relatively unspoiled havens for many species endemic to this part of the world. They also have a very long history of geographic isolation from each other and mainland New Zealand, and contain some of the least modified landforms in the world.

The island groups — Snares, Auckland, Bounty, Antipodes and Campbell — have a fascinating human history, with the results of both early Maori and European attempts at settlement and exploitation still visible.

The first of the islands to be protected as a nature reserve was Adams Island, the second largest of the Auckland Islands group,

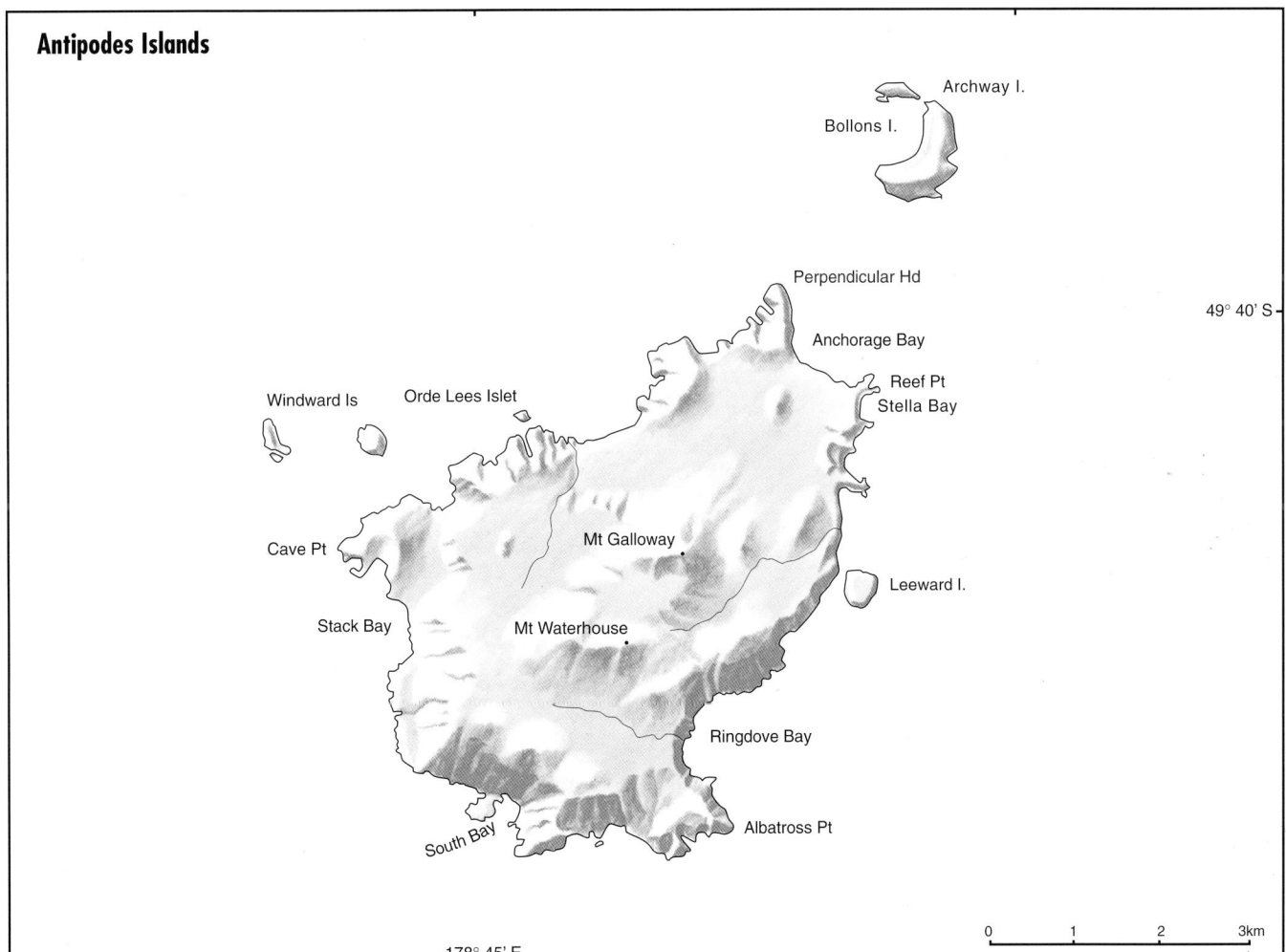

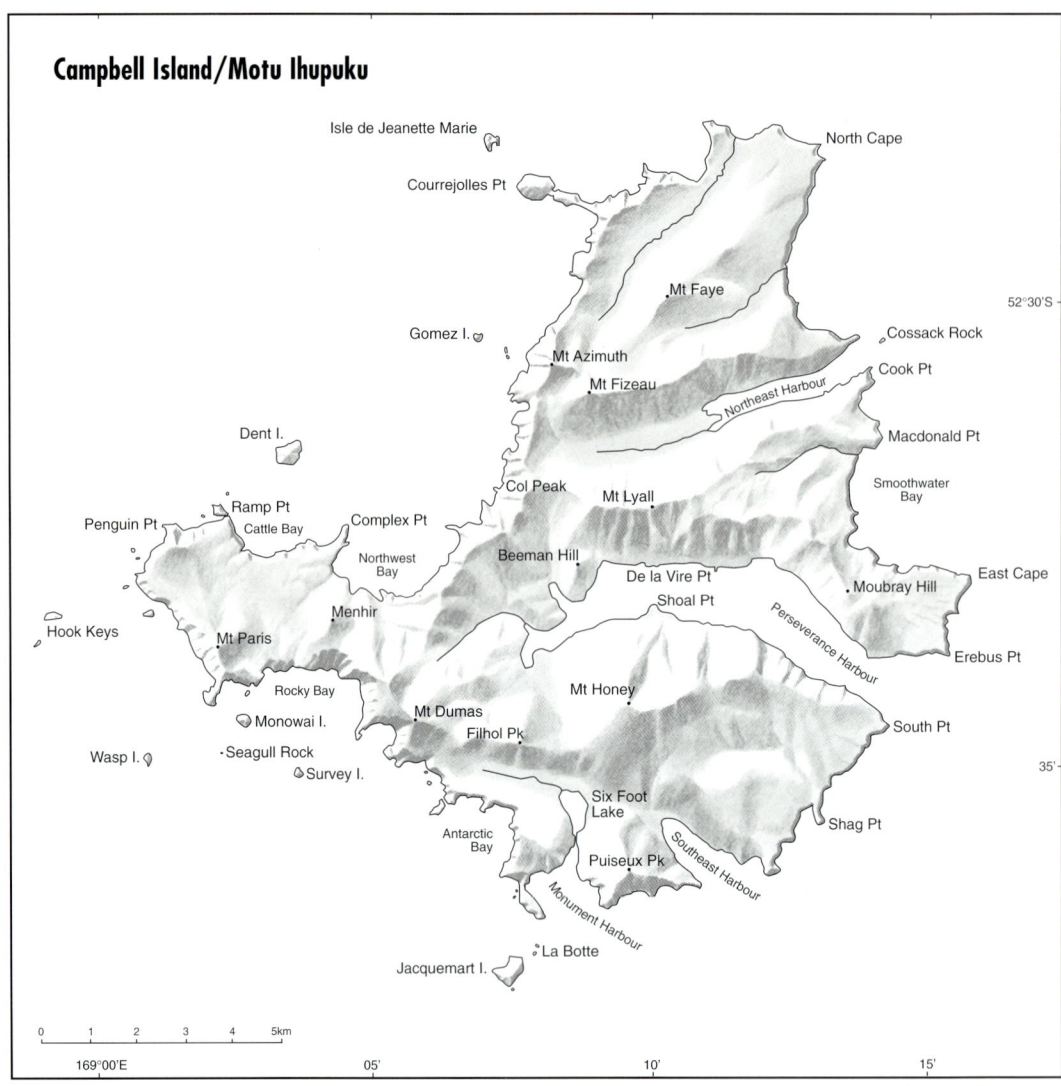

which was gazetted in 1910. The rest of the Auckland Islands were gazetted as nature reserves in 1934. Campbell Island followed in 1954, and the Antipodes, Snares and Bounty Islands in 1961.

Their declaration in 1986 as National Nature Reserves (under the Reserves Act 1977) and as a World Heritage Area in 1998, gives them the highest possible conservation status. Recognition by UNESCO's World Heritage Committee is only given to outstanding examples of evolutionary or biological history, or significant natural habitats where threatened species of animals or plants of universal value survive.

The Department of Conservation's principal management requirement is to preserve and maintain the native plant and animal species, ecosystems and environments of the islands. To achieve this goal the department sets strict guidelines for tourist visits to the islands.

Those who do not have the opportunity to visit the islands are able to gain an insight into the subantarctic by visiting the Roaring Forties Experience subantarctic gallery in the Southland Museum and Art Gallery, Invercargill, which was opened by Sir Edmund Hillary in 1998.

The International Setting

Position and sovereignty

New Zealand's five subantarctic island groups lie scattered across the Southern Ocean south and east of the South Island. The Antipodes are the most remote group, being 872 kilometres southeast of Bluff, the southernmost port of the South Island. The islands cover 2100 hectares and lie at latitude 49° 41´ south and longitude 178° 45´ east.

The smallest island group, the 135-hectare Bounty Islands, is 624 kilometres east of Bluff, at 47° 45´ south and 170° 02´ east. Only 209 kilometres from Bluff, at 48° 01´ south and 166° 36´ east, are the 328-hectare Snares Islands.

The largest group by far is the Auckland Islands, 465 kilometres south of Bluff. The main island covers 51,000 hectares, and Adams Island 10,117 hectares. They lie between 50° 30´

Courrejolles Peninsula, Campbell Island
CAROL WEST

and 50° 55´ south and 165° 50´ and 166° 20' east.

Campbell Island claims the most southerly location, 700 kilometres south of Bluff at 52° 35´ south and 169° 10´ east. It is an irregular shape, 16 kilometres by 16 kilometres, with an area of 11,331 hectares.

New Zealand's subantarctic islands are not alone in the Southern Ocean. South of the Subtropical Convergence — the northern limit of temperate waters — there are 22 major oceanic islands or island groups, containing 800 individual islands. These islands are administered as sovereign territories of: Norway — Bouvetøya; France — Ile Amsterdam, Ile St Paul, Iles Crozet and Iles Kerguelen; South Africa — Marion and Prince Edward Islands; Australia — Macquarie, Heard and McDonald Islands; United Kingdom — Gough Island and Tristan da Cunha.

Sovereignty of the Falkland Islands, South Georgia and South Sandwich Islands is claimed by both the United Kingdom and Argentina, while the South Orkney and South Shetland Islands are administered by international agreement under the Antarctic Treaty.

Biology

In a biogeographical sense, the New Zealand subantarctic islands occupy a cool-temperate zone: they lie between the Antarctic and Subtropical Convergences, have a mean annual temperature above 5°C, and support vegetation including trees and woody plants. They display biological differences from islands in the true subantarctic zone, which lie in the vicinity of the Antarctic Convergence, have a mean annual temperature of 1–5°C and no trees (e.g. South Georgia); and those in the Maritime Antarctic zone which have a mean annual temperature of less than 0°C and no flowering plants (e.g. Bouvetøya). Both physically and biologically, the New Zealand subantarctic islands are widely representative of their biogeographical realm, and are therefore of international significance.

The volcanic Auckland, Campbell and Antipodes Islands are important for unravelling the pattern of continental drift and the volcanic history of the southwest Pacific Basin. In contrast, The Snares and the Bounty Islands are granite masses, which reveal the character of the continental base-

Western Cliffs from South West Cape, looking towards Cape Lovitt, Auckland Islands
ANDRIS APSE

Anisotome latifolia
CRAIG POTTON

ment rocks making up the Campbell Plateau.

The high Auckland Island (the largest oceanic island in the Pacific subantarctic) and Campbell Island, although ice-free today, bear the striking imprint of Pleistocene glaciation.

The island biota is a culmination of a long history of geographic isolation, species dispersal, climatic factors, and community interaction without human interference until very recently. The evolution of this biota is of great international taxonomic and ecological interest, and the islands are of immense value for scientific study.

The distinctive island vegetation includes some of the southernmost forests in the world, species which are at the limit of their ecological tolerance, and many vascular (ferns and flowering) plants found nowhere else (endemics). The Auckland Islands support the richest floral assemblage of any island in the Southern Ocean with 233 taxa of vascular plants, including three species of *Pleurophyllum*, a genus endemic to the New Zealand subantarctic islands and Australia's Macquarie Island. Adams and Disappointment Islands in the Auckland Island group, and the whole Snares group, are among the last substantial land masses of the world harbouring vegetation largely unmodified by people and foreign animals. All the vegetated island groups have many plants that are considered to be rare, including 34 species on the Auckland Islands alone.

16   New Zealand's Subantarctic Islands

Below: New Zealand (Hooker's) sea lion
Greg Lind

Bottom: Royal albatrosses, Campbell Island
Chris Rance

Breeding grounds

As the only land masses in a vast expanse of the Southern Ocean, the islands are globally important as resting places and breeding grounds for thousands of marine mammals and countless numbers of seabirds. The populations of birds on the islands are huge. The Snares Group is estimated to harbour over six million breeding seabirds, comparable to the total number of seabirds around Great Britain and Ireland.

The Auckland Islands support the world's largest breeding populations of wandering albatross and shy mollymawk, while Campbell Island is home to the world's largest breeding population of royal albatross and the newly discovered Campbell Island snipe.

The Auckland Islands are also the principal breeding ground of one of the world's rarest seals, the New Zealand (Hooker's) sea lion.

History

Discovery

The islands may have been known to early Maori, but it was not until 1788 that the first of the five island groups was discovered by Europeans. These were the Bounty Islands, which were discovered by Captain William Bligh of mutiny on the *Bounty* fame. On 9 September 1788 he came across 'a cluster of small rocky islands' which he named 'after the ship, the Bounty Isles'. Then, on 23 November 1791, unbeknown to each other and on the same day, Captain George Vancouver of the *Discovery* and Lieutenant Broughton of the *Chatham* discovered The Snares.

On 26 March 1800, Captain Waterhouse of the *Reliance* sighted a group of islands which, because of their approximation to the antipodes of London, he named the 'Penantipodes'.

The Auckland Islands were not discovered by Europeans until 1806. On 18 August that year, Captain Abraham Bristow of the whaler *Ocean* sighted a group of islands which he named 'Lord Auckland's (my friend through my father)'.

The last of the five island groups, Campbell Island, was discovered on 4 January 1810 by Captain Frederick Hasselburgh of the sealer *Perseverance*, who named it after Robert Campbell, the owner of his sealing company. Sadly, Hasselburgh drowned in Perseverance Harbour. By an extraordinary coincidence the *Perseverance* itself was wrecked in the same harbour nineteen years later.

Following their discovery there was a rush of sealers to these subantarctic islands. However, with the wholesale slaughter of seals, the sealers soon all but exterminated their means of livelihood.

Antarctic explorers

During the year 1840, three famous Antarctic explorers anchored in Port Ross off the northeast tip of Auckland Island. The first to arrive was the American, Charles Wilkes, in the *Porpoise*. He found the harbour an excellent one in which to replenish wood and water, while his crew 'enjoyed themselves on chowders and fries.'

Only two days after Wilkes, the French expedition under Dumont d'Urville entered the harbour in the *Astrolabe* and the *Zelee*. D'Urville found the graves of some early whalers on Shoe Island, and his artist, Breton, has left us a fine painting of the island with the two ships anchored alongside.

By far the most significant of the three expeditions was the visit of the English naval vessels HMS *Erebus* and HMS *Terror* under the command of Captain James Ross (later Sir James). On board were two botanists Joseph Hooker (later Sir Joseph) and Dr David Lyall. They collected 80 flowering plants including the magnificent megaherbs, and many species which had never been described before. Later, Sir Joseph Hooker published details of the collection in his classic, *Flora Antarctica*.

Impressed by what later became known as Port Ross, James Ross carried out a hydrographic survey of the harbour. Then, before departing, he released several animals, including sheep, pigs, poultry and rabbits, and also planted a variety of vegetables and garden fruits as food for castaways.

Hardwicke

Fired by James Ross's report of an excellent harbour at Port Ross and his belief that it would serve as an ideal whaling base for the whole southern region, Charles Enderby, of the British whaling company Samuel Enderby & Son, determined to establish a whaling settlement at the port. In doing so he unwisely accepted, without question, the glowing account of Benjamin Morrell who, after a visit in 1829, reported that the 'Auckland Island is one of the finest places for a settlement. There are very few spots that could not be converted to excellent pasturage or tillage land.' Without bothering to check for himself, the gullible Enderby went ahead with his plans to found a settlement at Erebus Cove, Port Ross. 'The Auckland Islands are exceedingly healthy,' he enthused in his prospectus, 'and have a very rich virgin soil … The settler will be free from aboriginals, there being none on the island.'

Arriving at Port Ross in December 1849, the settlers were surprised to find over 60 Maori and Chatham Island Moriori people occupying the land. The Maori-Moriori party, under the chiefs Matioro and Manatere, had been on the island since 1842. Fortunately the two groups got on well, with the Polynesian settlers providing fish, birds and a meagre supply of vegetables from their gardens, as well as crew for the whaleboats. A large house was erected for Enderby, who had been elevated to the status of Lieutenant-Governor. Barracks, a storehouse, a jail (on Shoe Island), a chapel and cottages for the settlers were also built. On New Year's Day 1850 the settlement was formally named Hardwicke, in honour of the Earl of Hardwicke, the Governor of the company.

But things soon began to go very wrong for Charles Enderby, idealist that he was. Vegetables and crops failed to grow well in the acidic, peaty soil and too few whales were being caught to provide an income for the colony. In November 1850 the New Zealand Governor, Sir George Grey, arrived to pay an official visit, but he left feeling pessimistic about the settlement's future. By late 1851 the parent company in England was becoming deeply concerned about the total lack of revenue from whaling, and two special commissioners were sent out to enquire into the affairs of the establishment, and if necessary close the station down. At first the Lieutenant-Governor vehemently resisted their efforts to relieve him of his position, but he finally complied and returned to England. By 1852 the last of the settlers had departed.

Today the only two buildings at Erebus Cove are the boatshed, which still stands, and the collapsed remains of the castaway depot, both built after the settlement was abandoned. Further along the coast, in the rata forest, are the remains of the hut sites

History 19

and cobbled paths of Hardwicke. The 'Victoria Tree' was carved during a visit by HMCS *Victoria* in search of castaways, and the flagstaff was erected by the crew of the *Amherst* to replace the original Hardwicke flagmast. Half of the known graves in the Hardwicke cemetery are those of shipwrecked mariners. The most poignant reminder of the settlement is the headstone of Isabel Younger, who died on 19 November 1850, aged three months.

Shipwrecks

With the notable exception of the *Perseverance* and three ships lost on the Antipodes Islands, most shipwrecks that have been recorded occurred on the Auckland Islands. At least eight ships ended their days on the rugged reefs and cliffs of the Auckland Islands and over 100 lives were lost. The firsthand accounts of the survivors and how they eked out an existence on these cold, inhospitable islands until rescue finally came stir the imagination.

Grafton
The *Grafton* was driven aground in Carnley Harbour during a violent storm in January 1864. Captain Thomas Musgrave and his four companions all managed to struggle ashore and for over a year they lived in a crude hut which they called 'Epigwaitt' (Indian for 'dwelling by water'). Fortunately they were able to save the ship's dinghy and Musgrave, Raynal (a French adventurer) and one of the crew set out on an epic voyage to Stewart Island, which they reached safely five days later. Barely recovered, Musgrave returned in the rescue ship to pick up the two remaining castaways.

HMCS *Victoria* Post Office at Port Ross, Auckland Island
BURTON BROTHERS COLLECTION, MUSEUM OF NEW ZEALAND TE PAPA TONGAREWA, C.10566

Invercauld
The *Invercauld* was wrecked on the western cliffs of Auckland Island in May 1864. Nineteen of the crew of 25 managed to get ashore but only Captain Dalgarno, the first mate and a seaman survived the year that followed. They were eventually picked up from Enderby Island by the Spanish brig *Julian*. John Mahoney, the second mate, is

20 New Zealand's Subantarctic Islands

Fingerpost, Enderby Island, Auckland Islands
PETE MCCLELLAND

buried in the cemetery at Hardwicke where his tombstone still stands.

General Grant

Probably the most famous wreck of all was the *General Grant*, which drifted into a cavern in the western cliffs of Auckland Island in 1856. The foremast was driven through the hull when it struck the roof of the cavern and 68 people drowned as the ship sank. The fifteen survivors set out for Disappointment Island in two of the ship's boats, where they sheltered for two days before continuing on to Port Ross. Four men set out in an open boat in a desperate bid to seek help, but they were never seen again. The remaining castaways were eventually rescued by the *Amherst* in 1868. Over the years there have been a number of searches for the remains of the *General Grant* and the gold that she was carrying, so far without success.

Derry Castle

The *Derry Castle* was wrecked on the north coast at Enderby Island in 1887. Only eight of the complement of 23 were able to make it to shore, and the dead were buried in a mass grave. For a time the survivors lived in tussock huts. They later constructed a punt to cross to the castaway hut at Erebus Cove, where they were eventually found by the sealer *Awarua*. The figurehead from the *Derry Castle*, which for a time stood over the mass grave, is now in the Canterbury Museum. The punt has recently been brought out to the Southland Museum.

Cemetery, *Derry Castle* wreckage, Enderby Island, January 1888
BURTON BROTHERS COLLECTION, MUSEUM OF NEW ZEALAND TE PAPA TONGAREWA, C.15015

Dundonald

The barque *Dundonald* was wrecked on the coast at Disappointment Island in 1907. Twelve of the crew were drowned in the surf. The survivors erected grass huts in which they existed through the winter until becoming desperate, they constructed a flimsy coracle out of branches and seal skins in which they were able to cross to the main island and reach the depot at Erebus Cove. They were eventually rescued by the *Hinemoa* and the coracle was brought out to the Canterbury Museum. Jabez Peters, the mate, lies buried in the Hardwicke cemetery. After the earlier wrecks, castaway huts were erected on all the New Zealand subantarctic islands and these were serviced regularly by government steamers until 1927. The oldest of these huts still standing is the Stella Hut at Sandy Bay on Enderby Island. Built in 1880 by Captain McKenzie of the *Stella*, it replaced an earlier hut that was destroyed by fire.

Totorore

In June 1999 the yacht *Totorore* was due to call at Antipodes Island to pick up a party who had been studying albatross. The 11-metre twin-keel yacht failed to arrive. On June 21 searchers discovered wreckage from

Stella hut, Enderby Island, Auckland Islands
CRAIG POTTON

the Auckland-built yacht in South Bay, but no trace of her owner/skipper Gerry Clark (72) or his crewman Roger Sales (49) was found.

Farming

Auckland Islands

In 1894 the Auckland Islands were divided into three pastoral runs and offered for lease. W.J. Moffett took up his lease and in 1895 landed nine cattle and twenty sheep on Enderby Island. The remainder of Moffett's wild cattle on Enderby Island have since been removed.

Adams Island was also farmed for a short time. G.S. Fleming established a homestead in Carnley Harbour in 1900, landing 2000 sheep. However, the sheep gradually perished and Fleming forfeited his lease in 1910. In 1934 the whole island group was reserved for the preservation of its flora and fauna.

Campbell Island

With less scrub and more tussockland, Campbell Island proved to be a better proposition for farming than the Auckland Islands. In 1895 J. Gordon took up the lease of Campbell Island for a sheep run, building a homestead and woolshed at Tucker Cove in Perseverance Harbour, and releasing 300–400 sheep on the island. In 1900 Gordon sold out to Captain W.H. Tucker but remained as manager. With help from the shore whalers during their off-season, sheep farming continued on Campbell Island until 1931. Four thousand sheep and a few cattle were abandoned on the island. It was declared a nature reserve in 1954, and in 1970 and 1984 dividing fences were erected across the island to restrict the destruction of the vegetation by sheep. The remaining wild sheep were removed in 1990. The site of the homestead and woolshed is still evident at Tucker Cove.

Shore Whaling

With the decline of whaling in Cook Strait and the offer of work on Tucker's station, a party of Tory Channel whalers under Jack Norton set up a whaling station at Northwest Bay on Campbell Island in 1909. Using an open whaleboat, the party caught thirteen whales in the first season and hauled them ashore with a ship's windlass (a horizontal hauling winch) in what later became Capstan Cove. They continued to hunt with success until 1916 when the whole complement of the station, including the five Norton brothers, enlisted for the First World War. The remains of the windlass can still be seen at Capstan Cove. (Some seamen use the name capstan for both a capstan, which has a vertical hauling drum, and a windlass, which has a horizontal hauling drum.)

Following Norton's success, in 1911 H.F. Cook, from the Bay of Islands, established a whaling station at Northeast Harbour on Campbell Island. Cook's party also caught thirteen whales in their first season but the station closed down with the advent of the First World War in 1914. Three tripots and other relics can still be seen at the head of Northeast Harbour.

The Scientists

Both Germany and France sent expeditions to the New Zealand subantarctic islands to observe the transit of Venus in 1874. The Germans chose the Auckland Islands, setting up their observatory at Terror Cove in Port Ross. They were lucky, as the clouds cleared at the critical time of the transit, before later closing in again. The three brick pillars used for mounting their instruments remain at Terror Cove.

The French sent their expedition in the *Vire*, under Captain J. Jacquemart, to Campbell Island where they established their observatory at Venus Bay in Perseverance Harbour. Unfortunately they only caught a glimpse of Venus as it began to cross the sun. Nevertheless they made a thorough survey of the island and a number of their French place-names can be found on the map. The exact position of the grave of M. Duris, who died on the expedition and was buried on Point Duris, remained a mystery for some time, but it has recently been rediscovered. There are no remains of the observation station at Venus Cove.

Over the years many eminent scientists have visited and studied the islands, including Sir James Hector, Thomas Kirk, Sir William Benham, Leonard Cockayne, Sir Charles Fleming and Sir Robert Falla. The last two were members of the famous 'Cape Expedition' which was sent to coast-watch in the islands during the Second World War. Warned by the German government that war was imminent, the German steamer *Erlangen* had slipped quietly out of Dunedin Harbour in late August 1939. Captain Grams had only five days' fuel aboard and he headed for the Auckland Islands in the hope of finding firewood. Rata logs were cut and loaded aboard in Carnley Harbour and the *Erlangen* continued on her way. After this incident it was decided to mount a coastal watch in the islands and volunteers were called for. A

Tripots, Snares Islands
PETE MCCLELLAND

Coast-watcher's station, Tucker Cove, Campbell Island
CAROL WEST

Old stove, Tucker Cove, Campbell Island
CAROL WEST

number of leading scientists were included in the party, which was given the code name 'Cape Expedition'. The expedition was taken down in the *Tagua* in 1941, and coast-watching stations were established at Tagua Bay in Carnley Harbour, Ranui Cove at Port Ross, and Tucker Cove in Perseverance Harbour. The ketch *Ranui* was provided to act as a link between the stations.

Although the watch was discontinued at the end of the war the Tucker Cove base was kept open to act as a weather station. However, the base had been deliberately built back from the harbour to avoid detection and was in an unsuitable position for a modern meteorological base. A new station was constructed on Beeman Point, opened in 1957 and operated until 1995. Today the three Cape Expedition stations are derelict and two of the lookout huts, at Ranui Cove and Tagua Bay in Carnley Harbour, are being preserved by the Department of Conservation.

Geology

New Zealand's subantarctic islands are scattered across the Campbell Plateau, a submerged portion of the New Zealand continental landmass. Before the southwest Pacific Ocean began to form during continental drifting some 80 million years ago (80 Ma), the plateau was connected to Antarctica and formed part of the supercontinent of Gondwanaland. Crucial information from the rocky outcrops of the subantarctic islands, together with dredge samples, oil exploration drillholes, and seismic, gravity and magnetic surveys from ships and satellites, has enabled geologists to reconstruct this part of the Gondwana jigsaw puzzle.

Basement rocks beneath the plateau include granite, schist and greywacke that are of Mesozoic or older age (more than 100 million years old, or 100 Ma), similar to the rocks of Fiordland, Westland and Nelson, Marie Byrd Land in Antarctica, and parts of eastern Australia. Basement rocks are exposed on the Bounty, Campbell, Snares, and Auckland

Pegmatite veins (pale) cutting muscovite granite at Ho Ho Bay, Northeast Island, Snares group; a sleeping fur seal provides scale. The granite of the Bounty Islands has a similar appearance.
IAN TURNBULL

Island groups, and can be found as fragments on the Antipodes.

Overlying the basement of most of the Campbell Plateau is a blanket of sediments of Mesozoic to Cenozoic age (90–10 Ma), which has been mapped by seismic surveys and tested for oil and gas in several drillholes, mainly closer to New Zealand in a region known as the Great South Basin. The sediments are up to 5 km thick in the Great South Basin, but only a few hundred metres of these sediments are exposed on land, on the Auckland Islands and on Campbell Island.

The Auckland, Campbell, and Antipodes Island groups are primarily volcanic in origin, similar to the Dunedin, Lyttelton and Chatham Island volcanic centres to the north. The volcanic rocks range from mid-Cenozoic (25 Ma) on the Auckland Islands to Quaternary (0.5–1 Ma) on the Antipodes. The volcanic activity across the South Island, and the Campbell Plateau, built broad but isolated piles of lava flows, ash and scoria and is 'within-plate', rather than the result of plate boundary processes that make chains of volcanoes such as those in the North Island of New Zealand. Macquarie Island, to the southwest, is geologically quite different and lies on an upthrust mid-oceanic ridge of volcanic rock.

The Auckland Islands and Campbell Island were glaciated during the Quaternary ice ages (1 Ma to 15,000 years ago) and their eastern harbours are glacial fiords. Cirques and glacial moraines are present on both groups. All the subantarctic islands have been dramatically influenced and shaped by

Lichen zonation, Perseverance Harbour, Campbell Island
Carol West

Geology 27

ongoing marine erosion, which has produced the magnificent stacks, arches and huge cliffs typical of these Southern Ocean islands.

The Snares

The main Snares Islands, together with the Western Chain, are composed entirely of basement rocks; 100–120 Ma muscovite granite similar to that on nearby Stewart Island. There are rare pegmatite veins (coarser grained versions of the same granite), and on the Western Chain some blocks of schist have been caught up in the granite intrusion. The Traps, lying east of Stewart Island and north of The Snares, are also formed of muscovite granite, recently dated as 120 Ma.

Auckland Islands

The Auckland Islands are dominated by two overlapping shield volcanoes centred on Disappointment Island in the north (the Ross Volcano) and on Carnley Harbour in the south (Carnley Volcano); the majestic cliffs on the west of the main island clearly showing the interfingering lava flows from both volcanoes. Both the Ross and Carnley

Glacial moraines forming the 'arms' and seat of a cirque on the north side of Adams Island. Stacked lava flows, from the Carnley Volcano, which appear at the head of the cirque are typical of much of the Auckland Islands landscape.
IAN TURNBULL

Opposite: Basalt pillars, Enderby Island, Auckland Islands
LOU SANSON

volcanoes have been deeply eroded by glaciers on the eastern side of the island, and by the sea on the west, with Disappointment Island being the central remnant of the Ross Volcano.

The Carnley Volcano forms a large caldera, or volcanic depression, centred on Musgrave Peninsula and Circular Head, and is built up of at least 30 lava flows from 15 to 20 million years old. At Crab Bay, small areas of slightly older lavas (20–25 Ma) are intruded by many volcanic dikes. In the very centre of the caldera on Musgrave Peninsula the underlying basement rocks can be seen, consisting of biotite granite (95 Ma) which is also cut by many volcanic dikes. At Camp Cove a coarse conglomerate underlies the volcanics; pebbles in the conglomerate consist of volcanic rocks, and basement schists and granites. On the east side of Musgrave Peninsula are tiny remnants of fossiliferous marine sandstone and limestone, resting on the granite and immediately underneath the oldest lava flows. Intruded into the centre of the Carnley Volcano at Circular Head around 17 Ma, before it was eroded, is a pluton of coarse gabbro.

The Ross Volcano was centred on Disappointment Island; the underlying basement (or sedimentary) rocks are not exposed. The Ross Volcano is slightly younger (15–10 Ma) than the Carnley Volcano, and consists of up to 25 lava flows which are visible in the cross-section of the volcano on the western cliffs. Several small parasitic volcanic centres have been built up on the eastern flank of the volcano, although the more spectacular hills such as Mt Eden and Dea's Head are intrusive plugs, with the surrounding lava flows eroded away. The extensive lava flows from the Ross Volcano underlie Enderby, Shoe and other islands of Ross Harbour, and show very good columnar jointing.

The main island has been heavily glaciated. The harbours and inlets on the eastern coast are fiords, and the heads of most valleys, including Fly Harbour and Lake Turbott on Adams Island, contain glacial 'armchair' cirques. Lakes Speight, Tutanekai and Hinemoa lie in other cirques, ponded behind small moraine ridges. Prominent lateral moraine ridges mark the sites of old tributary glaciers falling into Carnley Harbour from Adams Island.

In several places on the eastern coast, and especially on Enderby Island, are deposits of morainic gravels and sands formed adjacent to the Auckland Island glaciers, and in places peat and lignite deposits are preserved within them. On several spurs on the eastern coast, old cliffs at around 40 metres above sea level reflect a Quaternary interglacial period when sea levels were much higher. On the western coast, upper sloping cliffs (probably formed earlier in the Quaternary period) are being actively truncated by the present-day lower vertical sea cliffs.

Campbell Island

Like the Carnley Volcano, Campbell Island is a glacially eroded remnant of a shield volcano, built on basement rocks overlain by a thin veneer of sediments.

The basement consists of metamorphosed mica schist, dated as Paleozoic (450 Ma), and closely resembling schists on the west coast of the South Island. The schists are exposed at Complex Point, and (very poorly) in the southwest corner of Perseverance Harbour. Also exposed along the northwest coast, and in the western coves of Perseverance Harbour, is a sedimentary sequence ranging from Cretaceous to middle Cenozoic (90–30 Ma in age), and

consisting of conglomerates, siltstones, sandstones and a distinctive cream-coloured limestone. The conglomerates are non-marine, formed of quartz gravels and including fossilised logs. The overlying sediments are marine and include siltstones which cross the Cretaceous-Tertiary boundary at 78 Ma. The distinctive Tucker Cove limestone forms cliffs on the western coast, and wide intertidal platforms around Tucker Cove. In places it includes very hard, brown flint nodules.

Overlying the limestone are younger (Miocene) marine ash and scoria deposits which mark the beginning of Campbell Island volcanism. Lava flows form the

A columnar jointed lava flow, draped and overlain by younger volcanic ash and scoria at Anchorage Bay, Antipodes Island. The columnar jointing is typical of many lava flows, both here and on the Auckland Islands; the ash and scoria layers form much of the coastline of the Antipodes group.
IAN TURNBULL

southern and eastern cliffs and the spectacular offshore islands. The prominent Beeman Hill is a volcanic plug which is harder than the surrounding flows, and is the site of a strong magnetic anomaly. The Menhir is a gabbroic intrusion, similar to the Circular Head gabbro in Carnley Harbour. All the volcanic rocks are between 6 and 11 Ma in age. Volcanic dikes intrude all the older rocks, contrasting strongly with the pale limestone.

Some raised beach deposits and moraines have been recognised in Northeast Harbour, but glacial features are not as well preserved as on the Auckland Islands.

Previous page: Volcanic dike, Campbell Island
WYNSTON COOPER

Antipodes Islands

The Antipodes Islands are entirely volcanic in origin, although fragments of the underlying basement granite have been found as inclusions in volcanic breccias; this granite is dated at 120–140 Ma. Sedimentary sandstone and siltstone fragments also occur in the breccias.

The main island was formed during two volcanic periods. Older volcanic flows, volcanic ash and breccias are preserved on the southwest coast and around Perpendicular Head, and are dated as up to 5 Ma. These have been eroded and then overlain by younger volcanics; the contact is marked by a layer of old boulder beach deposits.

These older volcanics are overlain by more ash and lava flows which slope into the centre of the island and form the spectacular and inaccessible cliffs which ring the main island. Smaller volcanic centres of similar rocks form Windward, Leeward and Bollons Islands.

The youngest volcanic rocks form the central volcanic cone (Mt Waterhouse and Mt Galloway), as well as the columnar jointed basalt flows at Anchorage Bay, Crater Bay and Southwest Bay. These rocks are as young as 0.5 Ma.

Bounty Islands

The Bounties, like The Snares, are entirely basement rock. The Bounty Island basement is a biotite granite with occasional finer grained variations (for example on Prion Island) and has been dated at 180–190 Ma, similar to granites recently found on Stewart Island. There are rare dikes of darker plutonic rock of as yet unknown affinity.

Marine mudstone and harder pale-coloured Tucker Cove Limestone (right) at the head of Camp Cove, Perseverance Harbour, Campbell Island; the Cretaceous-Tertiary time boundary occurs within the mudstone. These sediments are intruded by a much younger basalt dike (right foreground).
IAN TURNBULL

SOILS

With the exception of the Bounty Islands and adjacent small rock stacks, all the subantarctic islands are mantled by peaty soils which have evolved over thousands of years under the cool, moist climate of the Southern Ocean. The Bounty Islands are rock and bare of soil.

These peats are composed almost entirely of plant remains, and mineral matter is only important in small areas such as the sand dunes of Enderby Island, or where soils are shallow. Peat thickness is strongly influenced by slope, and flat or gently sloping areas may be blanketed by up to five metres of peat. On steep slopes only 1–2 metres of peat may have developed, and this has often collapsed as landslides — frequently involving fragments of underlying rocks.

Soil textures range from friable with obvious plant remains to soapy or greasy with plants strongly decomposed. Near coastlines or streams, sand and pebbles, and occasionally bird and mammal skeletons, may be interlayered with peat.

Landsliding and tunnel gully erosion of peat (often with gullies several metres deep) are natural phenomena and ongoing.

Peat profile on west side of Enderby Island, Auckland Islands
CAROL WEST

However, erosion by wind has been extensive on Campbell Island and to a lesser extent on the Auckland Islands, triggered by trampling and browsing of overlying vegetation by introduced animals. Some erosion is also due to the natural processes of nest construction by albatrosses and burrowing petrels. Peat deflation hollows on Campbell Island are often very moist and can be quite deep.

On the Bounty Islands, organic material can accumulate in cracks in the rock but never builds up because of the intense traffic of birds and fur seals. Rain also washes the built-up material out of the cracks.

Olearia forest, Snares Islands
BRIAN RANCE

CLIMATE

'Cold, wet and windy' would be a succinct description of subantarctic weather. However, this rather bleak tag belies the fact that occasional days of clear, calm weather are experienced on the islands.

Located between latitudes 47° and 53° south, the five island groups rise out of the Southern Ocean in a region overwhelmingly dominated by persistent westerly winds and cold fronts — known as the Roaring Forties and Furious Fifties. These westerly winds increase in intensity with increasing latitude, and are more frequent during spring than other seasons.

Measurements from the New Zealand Meteorological Service weather station at Beeman Point on Campbell Island show that wind gusts in excess of 63 kph (35 knots) occur on about 280 days per year. Gusts in excess of 96 kph (50 knots) occur on at least 100 days annually, and the mean hourly windspeed is about 32 kph.

Clear weather in this view to Dent Island from Penguin Bay, Campbell Island
LOU SANSON

Above: High winds on Adams Island
Lou Sanson

Left: Cloud cover near the top of Azimuth Saddle, Campbell Island
Carol West

Opposite: Cliffs, western Auckland Island
Lou Sanson

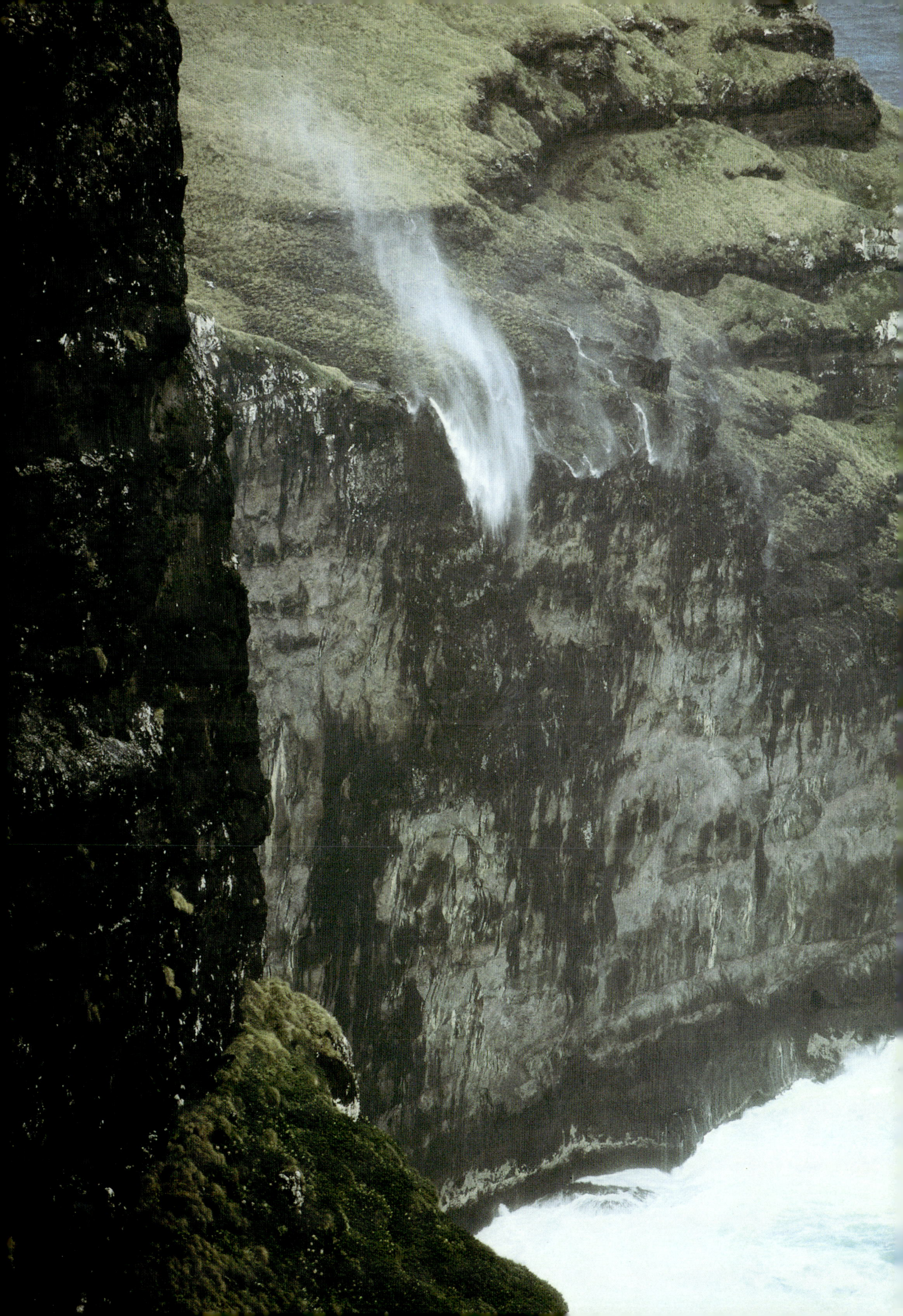

Snow near Carnley Harbour, Auckland Islands
LOU SANSON

South of New Zealand cloud cover increases markedly, and the annual sunshine total on Campbell Island is about 660 hours (16 percent of the possible amount). On mainland New Zealand, Invercargill can expect about 1620 hours, Christchurch about 2000 hours, and Auckland about 2100 hours per year.

While rainfall occurs on the islands on more than 300 days per year, the average annual total of 1360 mm recorded at Campbell Island is only 200–300 mm more than the totals recorded in Wellington and Auckland. Annual rainfall varies considerably among the five groups — Auckland Island has probably about double the amount of rain that falls on the Antipodes.

The rain usually occurs as drizzle or light rain with heavier falls during the frequent passage of cold fronts through the region. Thunder and lightning are uncommon, occurring on average on fewer than two days per year. Snow can fall during any month of the year, but it is usually light and does not tend to settle on the ground for lengthy periods.

Temperatures are cool, with mean annual temperatures varying from 11°C at The Snares to 6°C at Campbell Island. Temperatures do not usually rise much above 12°C, even during the summer months, while at the other end of the scale they do not sink much below 2°C. Extremes of 21°C and -7°C have been recorded at Campbell Island weather station.

Climate | 41

Sunset, Port Ross,
Auckland Island
BRIAN RANCE

Vegetation

The summer climate of New Zealand's subantarctic islands is as cool and windy as subalpine and alpine zones of the mainland, and there are low sunshine hours. This and the maritime influence are the major factors affecting vegetation patterns. The peaty, acidic, waterlogged soils reflect the cool, humid climate. Seabirds and other wildlife also have an important effect on vegetation, through trampling, burrowing and nutrient enrichment.

Only four of the five island groups are heavily vegetated. On the barren Bounty Islands only algae and lichens survive. Forest cover is restricted to The Snares, the Auckland Islands and sheltered parts of Campbell Island. Generally, maritime and upland areas are dominated by one or more of the tussock species (these are large tuft-forming grasses). Shrublands and herb moor (a mixture of stunted shrubs, cushion plants, tussocks and herbs) are also widespread. The highest peaks support alpine rushlands, cushion bogs and fellfields.

Hebe benthamii,
Auckland Islands
CHRIS RANCE

Vegetation   43

rata; blue in forget-me-not (*Myosotis antarctica, M. capitata*) and *Hebe benthamii*; and yellow in Maori onion (*Bulbinella rossii*) and the tree daisy (*Brachyglottis stewartiae*).

Left: *Stilbocarpa polaris*
CRAIG POTTON

The Snares

The Snares are the northernmost of the New Zealand subantarctic islands, and their milder climate is reflected in the tall vegetation that is found there.

Pleurophyllum hookerii
LOU SANSON

The subantarctic flora has four biogeographical elements: plants which are also found on the New Zealand mainland; plants which are found throughout the subantarctic zone (that is, circumpolar species); species and genera, such as *Pleurophyllum*, which are endemic to the New Zealand subantarctic islands (and Macquarie Island); and species which are endemic to individual island groups.

There are two special features of the subantarctic flora. Compared to New Zealand, plants have larger leaves and/or flowers, and exhibit a greater diversity of flower colour. 'Megaherbs' such as the large rhubarb-like punui (*Stilbocarpa polaris* and *S. robusta*) and the large-leaved, brightly flowered endemic daisies (*Pleurophyllum criniferum, P. hookerii* and *P. speciosum*) demonstrate these features well. Even species which are common on the New Zealand mainland tend to have larger leaves, for example, *Coprosma foetidissima*.

Large foliage is thought to be an adaptive response to cloudy, humid conditions and cool air temperatures. Whereas New Zealand flowers are typically pale (usually white) and small, subantarctic flowers show a range of colours from pink through mauve to red in *Pleurophyllum, Anisotome, Gentiana* and

Bulbinella rossii
CRAIG POTTON

The Snares are also the only island group with predominant forest cover. The tree daisy *Olearia lyallii* covers much of the island, with *Brachyglottis stewartiae* in more sheltered situations, and *Hebe elliptica* in the coastal zone. The coastal verge and exposed western side of the island are clothed with tussocks (*Poa tennantiana* and *P. astonii*).

The immense number of seabirds has a profound effect on the vegetation. Ground under the forest is largely bare and unstable because of the very high density of bird burrows, while Snares crested penguins create tracks and destroy vegetation around their nesting colonies.

The flora of The Snares consists of a meagre 22 species of flowering plants and ferns, including only three woody species. The Snares are one of the most pristine subantarctic island groups, with only two introduced species of plant. The native carrot, *Anisotome acutifolia*, is the only species endemic to The Snares group, and it is uncommon. *Stilbocarpa robusta* is the only megaherb on The Snares.

Because of the close proximity of Stewart Island, there are strong botanical links to southern New Zealand (that is, the sharing of *Poa tennantiana*, *Brachyglottis stewartiae*, *Asplenium scleroprium* and other species). A distinct form of the threatened Cook's scurvy grass (*Lepidium oleraceum*), so named because it was collected and brewed by Captain Cook to prevent scurvy in his crew, is found on the island. This species was once widespread along the coast of mainland New Zealand, but because of its palatability to introduced mammals it is now largely restricted to offshore islands.

Antipodes Islands

The Antipodes Islands are predominantly covered by grasslands interspersed with patches of *Coprosma rugosa* var. *antipoda* shrubland, gullies of tall, prickly shield fern and, particularly where seabirds have opened up areas, patches of low herbs and shorter grasses.

The coastal fringe of Antipodes Island consists of dense, tall tussocks of *Poa foliosa* and *P. litorosa* and large areas of razor-edged *Carex* species. The abundant seabird burrows and the two metre height of the plants make it difficult to penetrate this vegetation. Exposed parts of the coast have a low vegetation of herbs including striking green cushions of *Colobanthus muscoides*. Larger herbs such as the nettle (*Urtica australis*), *Stilbocarpa polaris* and the Antipodes carrot (*Anisotome antipoda*) occur among the coastal tussocks.

The inland plains afford easier travel, with shorter and more widely spread tussocks of *Poa litorosa*. Mats of *Coprosma perpusilla* are dominant intertussock species, while the bidi-bid, *Acaena minor*, and *Gentiana antipoda* are also common. Megaherbs such as *Pleurophyllum criniferum*, *Anisotome antipoda* and *Stilbocarpa polaris* are also present. The large, endemic *Senecio antipodus* is often present in areas opened up by seabirds, and it is typically covered with black, hairy magpie moth larvae, which can completely defoliate it. Generally, taller tussock, fern and scrub covers the slopes of the higher hills of the main island. Vegetable garden-like associations of megaherbs are a special feature of the wetter sites, while recent large slips are covered by white lichens.

Seventy-one species of vascular plants are recorded on the islands, of which four species are introduced. The four introduced

Top: *Stilbocarpa polaris*
CAROL WEST

Below: *Gentiana* sp.
LINDSAY CHADDERTON

species remain very local in occurrence, and are generally found close to the hut or some penguin colonies. Four plant taxa are endemic to the islands; *Gentiana antipoda*, *Coprosma rugosa* var. *antipoda*, *Senecio antipodus* and a variety of chickweed, *Stellaria decipiens* var. *angustata*. The present lack of large browsing mammals contributes to a lush vegetation with natural communities in excellent condition (mice are the only introduced mammal).

Forest, shrubland and tussock, Auckland Island
LINDSAY CHADDERTON

Auckland Islands

Auckland Island is the largest of New Zealand's subantarctic islands, and this is reflected in the diversity of its vegetation. There are distinct altitudinal zones in the vegetation, although some zones are somewhat condensed. In the salt spray zone of the most exposed sites there is often a herb turf. Above it, in exposed sites, is a tussockland of *Poa litorosa* and/or *P. foliosa* with associated herbs.

Beyond the coastal zone, in more sheltered sites of the north and east, is a dwarfed forest dominated by southern rata (*Metrosideros umbellata*, the same species as in the South and Stewart Islands). When in full flower the rata gives an impressive show of red. Underneath, the many twisted and gnarled stems give the forest a haunted atmosphere. Locally dominant, around Ewing Island and Erebus Cove, are forests of the tree daisy, *Olearia lyallii*. This species appears to have colonised Auckland Island in the last 200 years and may have dispersed naturally from The Snares. Both these forest types are very simple, with few understorey shrubs and ground cover plants, although mosses and liverworts may carpet the floor.

Above the taller forest is a very dense subalpine shrubland zone of *Dracophyllum*, *Coprosma*, *Myrsine* and rata, often forming a mosaic with open herb-moor vegetation. The moor is low in stature and easy to travel through. It is also one of the most diverse communities, with a mixture of dwarfed woody species, herbs, tussocks, ferns and mosses. Some of the special features are the hard cushions of *Oreobolus pectinatus* and *Phyllachne colensoi*, upon which grows the small and brightly coloured *Gentiana concinna*.

Vegetation   47

Rata
LINDSAY CHADDERTON

The wet, peaty alpine tops support an extensive tussock landscape, dominated by *Chionochloa antarctica* (a relative of mainland snow tussocks). Hidden among the tussocks are the purple and white flowered daisy *Damnamenia vernicosa*, the blue-flowered shrub *Hebe benthamii*, the mauve-flowered *Gentiana concinna*, as well as many lichens. Scattered rock outcrops dotted along the ridges harbour a unique assemblage of

Mosses under rata trees, Auckland Islands
WYNSTON COOPER

Top: *Pleurophyllum speciosum* and *Anisotome antipoda*, Adams Island, Auckland Islands
CRAIG POTTON

Below: *Bulbinella rossii*, *Pleurophyllum speciosum* and *Anisotome latifolia*
CRAIG POTTON

plants. These, like coastal cliffs, provide refuge from browsing animals for many plants, including the megaherbs *Pleurophyllum* spp., *Stilbocarpa polaris* and *Anisotome antipoda*. The highest, most exposed alpine tops support a sparsely vegetated fellfield community dominated by mosses.

Introduced animals have had a profound impact on the vegetation. Pigs and goats have removed the megaherbs from accessible sites on Auckland Island. Goats have been eradicated but pigs continue to modify the vegetation by rooting for invertebrates and plant roots as well as eating more palatable species.

Enderby Island has been substantially modified by farming in the past, and considerable areas of rata forest have been replaced by a shrubland/moor mosaic. Until 1993, rabbits and cattle continued to influence the vegetation of Enderby, creating meadows of the (unpalatable) *Bulbinella rossii* which produce a mass of yellow flowers in late October/early November — a feature of the island at present. Since these browsers have been removed, many plant species which were suppressed have begun to expand their ranges to form distinctive herbfield communities, especially in the coastal zone; for example the megaherbs *Anisotome latifolia* and *Stilbocarpa polaris*, and tussocks of *Chionochloa antarctica* and *Poa litorosa*.

Within the Auckland Islands the only sizeable dune area is Sandy Bay on Enderby Island. At present, vegetation zones on Enderby comprise a coastal zone of herb turf or tussockland, depending on degree of exposure; rata forest; shrublands comprising *Dracophyllum*, rata, *Coprosma* and *Myrsine*; and a herb moor of cushion plants including *Gentiana concinna*. These patterns are expected to change as the island continues to recover from the impact of browsing mammals.

The zonation on Adams Island is similar to that on Auckland Island except that the rata forest is limited to sheltered sites on the northern side of the island. Tussocklands are extensive. Only on Adams Island and

Vegetation   49

some of the other offshore islands can the full selection of megaherbs be seen at their glorious best.

The Auckland Island group has the richest flora of the New Zealand subantarctic islands; 233 taxa have been recorded, 196 of which are native. Thirteen of the European introductions still persist around disturbed sites.

The islands claim six endemic taxa including two gentians (*Gentiana concinna* and *G. cerina*), a buttercup (*Ranunculus subantarcticus* subsp. *subantarcticus*), a stinging nettle (*Urtica aucklandica*), a plantain (*Plantago aucklandica*) and a grass (*Poa aucklandica* subsp. *aucklandica*), all closely related to species on the New Zealand mainland. The soft tree fern *Cyathea smithii* grows on the Auckland Islands, which is the most southern locality for tree ferns in the world.

Above: *Anisotome latifolia*
CRAIG POTTON

Below: *Ranunculus pinguis*, Adams Island, Auckland Islands
PETE MCCLELLAND

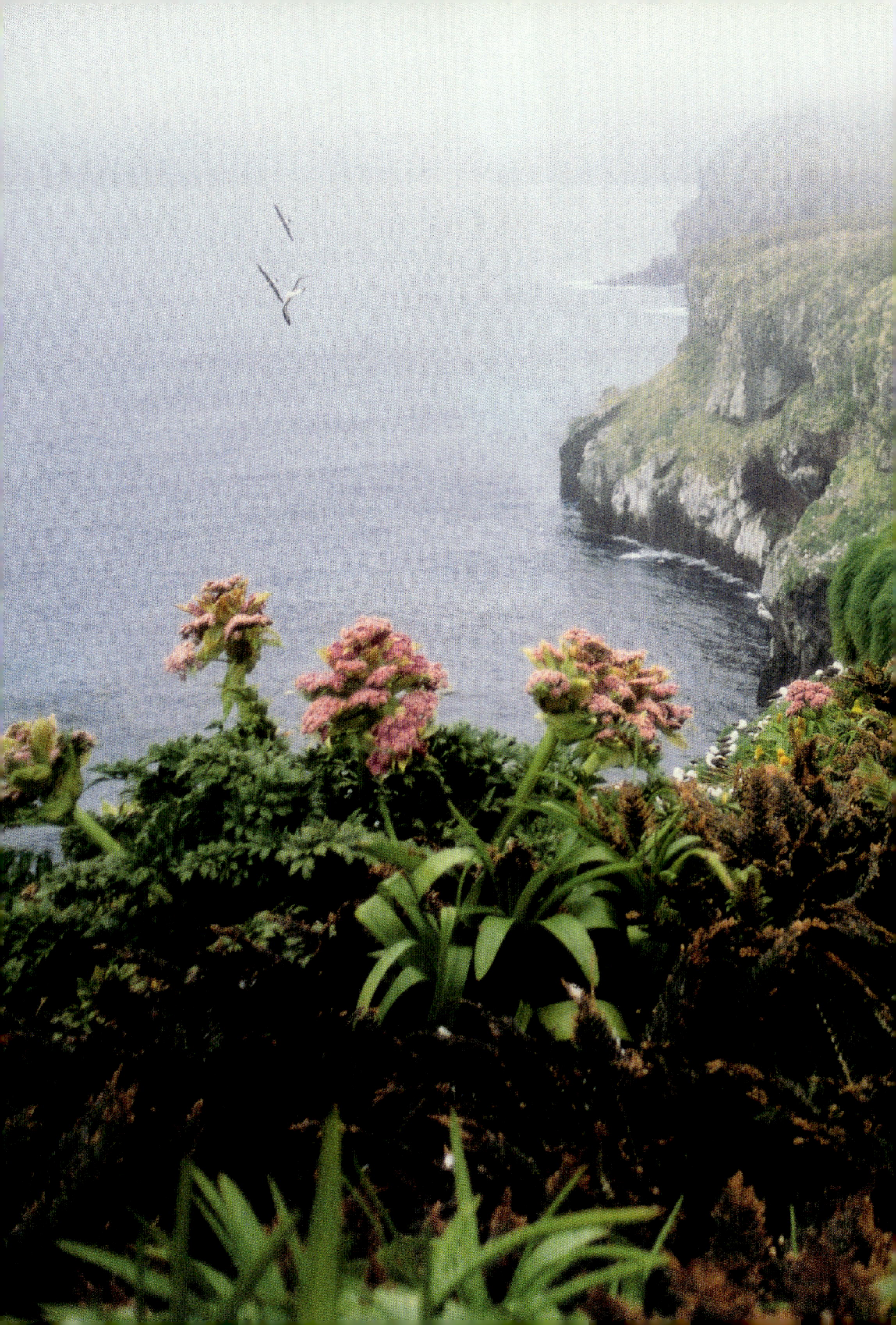

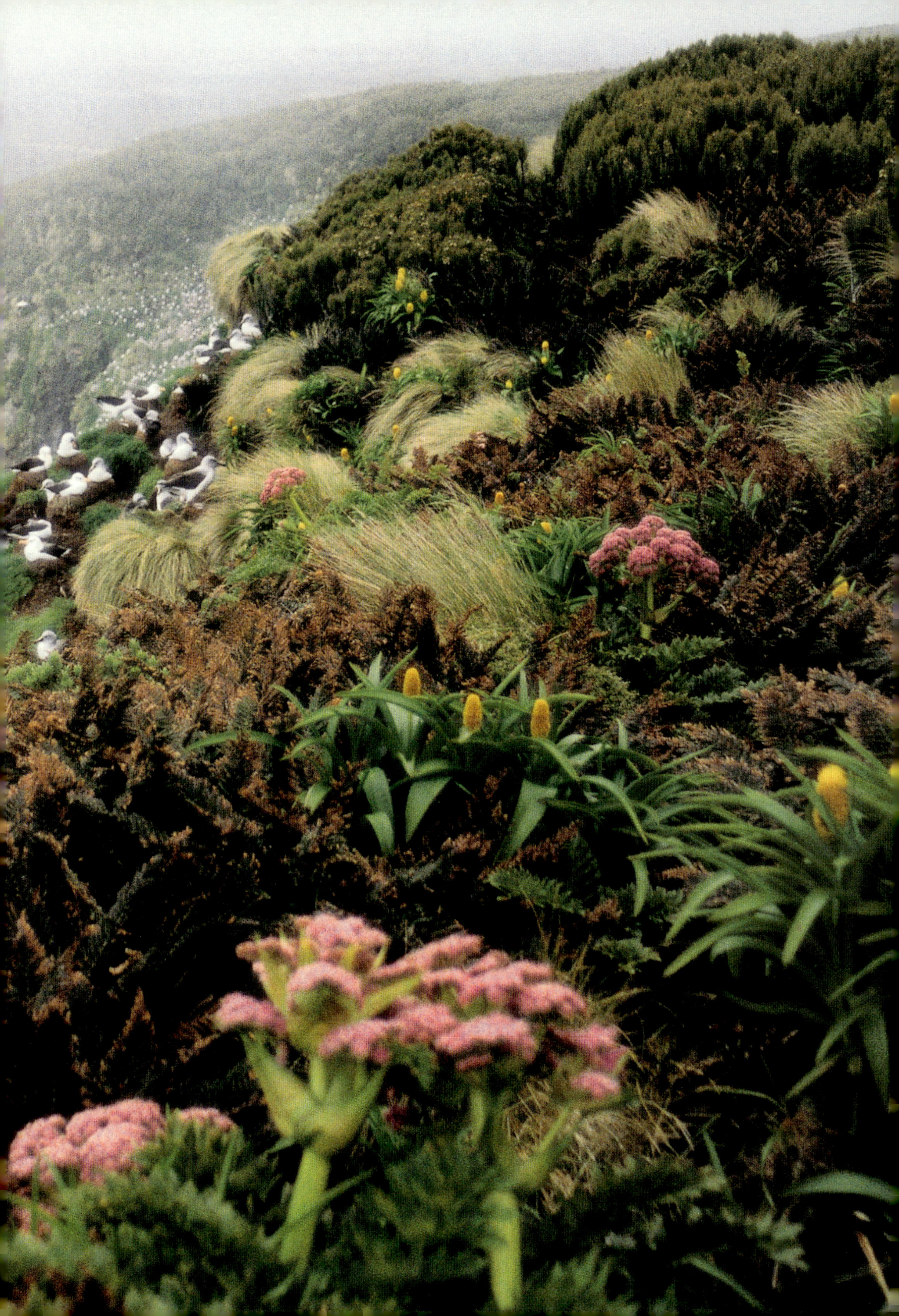

Previous page: Megaherbs, Bull Rock, Campbell Island
CAROL WEST

Campbell Island

The Campbell Island group is the most southern of New Zealand's subantarctic islands, and the vegetation reflects its harsh climate. The vegetation sequences are generally similar to the Auckland Islands, however the forest is even more dwarfed and lacking in diversity. Rata is not present.

Scattered along the shore in the spray zone is a coastal turf, and beyond this is tall *Poa litorosa* tussockland. Sheltered sites support a subalpine-like shrubland, or dwarf forest, dominated by *Dracophyllum scoparium* and *D. longifolium* with *Coprosma* species and weeping mapou (*Myrsine divaricata*). This shrubland is very dense, attaining five metres in height and extending to about 180 metres above sea level. There are also cushion bog lanes and mosaics of *Coprosma*, weeping mapou and fern in this area.

The uplands once supported tall *Chionochloa antarctica* snow tussockland, which was depleted as a result of sheep grazing and replaced by a grassy meadow dominated by *Poa litorosa*. However, sheep were exterminated in 1991 and the *Chionochloa* tussocks and *Hebe benthamii* are recovering at pace. Within this zone, the megaherbs which were much reduced by sheep are also recovering dramatically. Some areas now rival the famed Fairchild's Garden of Adams Island for their spectacular flower displays. *Pleurophyllum speciosum*, *Anisotome antipoda*, *A. latifolia* and *Stilbocarpa polaris* make up the main species in these megaherb meadows.

The high alpine areas are dominated by the rush *Marsippospermum gracile* and *Bulbinella rossii*. Wet drainage areas contain the rushes *Rostkovia magellanica* and *Juncus scheuchzerioides*, and cushion-forming plants.

The vascular flora consists of 213 species, of which 128 are native. There are six endemic taxa — a forget-me-not (*Myosotis antarctica*); a gentian (*Gentiana antarctica*);

Coastal zonation, Tucker Cove, Campbell Island
GREG LIND

Right: *Dracophyllum*
LINDSAY CHADDERTON

a daisy (*Damnamenia vernicosa* var. *mollicula*); two buttercups (*Ranunculus subscaposus* and *R. subantarcticus* subsp. *campbellensis*); and a grass (*Poa aucklandica* subsp. *campbellensis*).

Introduced plant species have minimal impact on native plants and animals. Most were introduced when the island was farmed, and they are most common around the settlement sites at the head of Perseverance Harbour and on disturbed ground near the now abandoned Meteorological Station at Beeman Point. Some, such as New Zealand flax (*Phormium tenax*), have been introduced from mainland New Zealand. Interestingly, a single spruce tree is present on the island. It has struggled to a height of about six metres and according to the *Guinness Book of Records* gained fame as the loneliest tree in the world.

Pleurophyllum speciosum, Campbell Island
CHRIS RANCE

INVERTEBRATES

The New Zealand subantarctic islands are home to a diverse and fascinating terrestrial invertebrate fauna, that is, insects, spiders, mites, snails and their kind. In contrast to the birds of the islands, which immediately impress with their size, familiarity and sheer force of numbers, the invertebrates tend to be relatively inconspicuous, favouring a concealed existence, away from the ravages of the subantarctic climate. These cryptic tendencies were emphasised by Krone, a photographer with the 1874 German transit of Venus expedition to the Auckland Islands, who commented, 'the world of insects seems like dead except for the extremely unpleasant sandflies [*Austrosimulium vexans*] and big blue blowflies [*Calliphora quadrimaculata*] which occur near the coast in millions …'

Insulanoplectron spinosum,
Snares Island
MIKE MEADS

Study of the subantarctic invertebrates dates back to collections made from the Auckland Islands during Dumont d'Urville's 'Voyage au Pole Sud' in 1840. Later that year, Sir James Clark Ross's British Antarctic Expedition visited and collected specimens from Auckland and Campbell Islands. From the late 1800s, several New Zealand scientists made collections during regular government trips to reprovision the islands' castaway depots. The first major New Zealand-based scientific study was the 1907 Philosophical Institute of Canterbury expedition, which visited all the islands, and included the well-known entomologist G.V. Hudson and zoologists C. Chilton and G.R. Marriner. Extensive collecting was also done during the Second World War's coast-watching 'Cape Expedition'. More recent studies include Bishop Museum of Hawaii expeditions to Auckland and Campbell Islands, and Canterbury University expeditions to Antipodes and Snares Islands. The Bounty Islands' fauna was only first seriously investigated in 1978. Knowledge of the subantarctic fauna remains far from complete and new species, and even new genera, continue to be discovered.

The subantarctic fauna is essentially of New Zealand origin and is a mixture of species from ancient and more recent dispersal events. Many of the species are subantarctic endemics, and are often endemic to the individual island groups. Several endemic genera exist, such as four cave weta genera, one from each of the Auckland, Bounty, Campbell and Snares Islands. Other species are shared with mainland New Zealand and some with the Chatham Islands. A few, like the intertidal ground beetle *Kenodactylus audouini*, have circumpolar or southern hemisphere distributions.

The size of the fauna is small compared with that of mainland New Zealand, but is consistent with the comparatively small land area, isolation and high latitude of the islands. The Auckland Islands have the largest fauna with about 450 arthropod species, including 24 spiders, 11 springtails and over 200 insects. Among the insects are 57 beetle species, 110 flies and 39 moths.

Mecodema alternans hudsoni, Snares Islands
MIKE MEADS

Hadramphus stilbocarpae, Snares Islands
MIKE MEADS

Next largest is the Campbell Island fauna with over 380 species, including two crustaceans, 90 spiders and mites, and over 200 insects. Up to 40 percent of these species are shared with the Auckland Islands.

The fauna of the Antipodes Islands includes around 100 insects and 17 spiders. About 17 percent of this fauna is endemic. Many species are common to the Auckland and Campbell Islands but five species are shared only with the Bounty Islands.

The barren and bleak Bounty Islands present a hostile environment, yet three spiders, 24 insects, several mites and collembola, and species of amphipod, isopod and land snail, live there. Around a third of the fauna is endemic. Most remarkable is a ground beetle, *Bountya insularis*. It is the only species in this endemic genus and is from a group not otherwise represented in the New Zealand fauna. Its nearest relatives live in Australia and South America.

The Snares Islands' fauna includes around 13 crustaceans and 132 insects. The fauna shows close links with Stewart Island and mainland New Zealand faunas. A knobbled weevil (*Hadramphus stilbocarpae*), for example, is also found on islands off Stewart Island and Fiordland.

The islands' invertebrates occur in a wide range of habitats. Many live in close association with birds, some relying on them directly, such as the parasitic lice, fleas and ticks. A range of herbivores, scavengers, predators and parasites live among nests, colonies and neighbouring guano-enriched plants. Further species have strong associations with the tussock grasslands, shrubs and trees. The megaherbs are hosts to a range of aphids, moths and weevils. The knobbled weevil feeds on *Stilbocarpa* and *Anisotome* on the Snares Islands. The Campbell Island ribbed weevil (*Heterexis seticostatus*) feeds on the native lily *Bulbinella rossii*. The boldly patterned, day-flying magpie moth (*Nyctemera annulata*) feeds on an endemic subspecies of *Senecio* on the Antipodes Islands.

On the seashore, rotting kelp is home to masses of scurrying, spider-like kelp flies which, on Auckland and Campbell Islands, include the giant, wingless *Baeopterus robustus*. Amphipods, rove and ground beetles can be found running among boulders on the beaches. The islands also support a small freshwater fauna, including species of midge, caddisfly, stonefly and, on the Auckland Islands, the only subantarctic mayfly, *Atalophlebioides aucklandensis*.

Flying is a risky strategy in the wind-swept subantarctic environment. Consequently, flightlessness is a common theme among the islands' insects. Flightless insects include *Antarctopria diomediae*, a tiny parasitic wasp endemic to the Bounty Islands; a semi-terrestrial stonefly, *Apteryoperla campbelli*, from Campbell Island; and a cranefly, *Erioptera antipodarum*, from the Antipodes Islands. About two-thirds of the moths and most of the beetles are wingless or have reduced wings.

Several invertebrate species have been introduced to the islands. Some of the highly mobile species such as aphids, thrips and spiders probably reached the islands on wind currents, but others have been introduced by humans. A few household pests, such as the brown house moth (*Hofmannophila pseudospretella*) and the Australian spider beetle (*Ptinus tectus*), were probably introduced with expedition supplies.

Of much greater concern is the presence of introduced mammals, principally rats on Campbell Island and mice on Antipodes and Auckland Islands. Large, flightless invertebrates, in particular, are easy prey to them. On Antipodes Island, mice have caused the extinction of a cave weta and an undescribed ground beetle, and have greatly reduced numbers of other vulnerable species. The giant weevil *Oclandius laeviusculus* has been eliminated by rats on Campbell Island but still exists on the tiny, rat-free Dent, Jacquemart and Monowai Islands. The same species may have been exterminated by mice on Auckland Island, but can be found on neighbouring, predator-free Adams Island. Predatory mammals continue to pose an enormous threat to the invertebrate fauna. Several species may be on the brink of extinction and others will surely be exterminated if further introductions occur. Perhaps most vulnerable is the giant weevil *Lyperobius nesidiotes*, whose total population is apparently restricted to a room-sized patch of *Anisotome* host plants on Broughton Island in the Snares group.

Oclandius laeviusculus, Ocean Island, Auckland Islands
MIKE MEADS

BIRDS

The initial and most lasting impression of New Zealand's subantarctic islands and their surrounding oceans is one of seabirds wheeling and soaring against stark, misty cliffs or effortlessly skimming over turbulent seas on long, narrow wings. More than 40 seabird species live here, from huge albatrosses to tiny petrels. There are also over 80 land-bird species which breed on, or at least regularly visit, the islands. The diversity of nesting seabirds and the frequent endemism in land-birds are features of the birdlife on these remote islands. The unique relationship which exists between the birds on the islands is shown most clearly on the Antipodes and Auckland groups. Here parakeets, which are usually tropical or subtropical species, live in close association with penguins, a subantarctic species.

Black-browed mollymawks
CRAIG POTTON

Isolation and the relatively small size of the five island groups has protected most of these birds from human colonisation and development. The exceptions are the two largest groups, Auckland and Campbell, which have been the most affected by introduced predatory mammals. Feral cats and pigs on Auckland Island and Norway rats and feral cats on Campbell Island have confined many of the smaller seabirds and endemic land-birds to the outlying islands within each group. It is on these small islands, and the less disturbed Snares, Antipodes and Bounty Islands, that the abundance, variety and tameness of sub-antarctic wildlife can be truly appreciated.

Because land masses are few and far between in the Southern Ocean, these islands are vital breeding grounds. Each year the urge to breed brings millions of seabirds to the islands. Most of these birds do not touch land between breeding seasons and, for some albatross species, this can mean several years at sea. It takes a full year for these very large birds to rear a single chick to independence so, at best, they only breed every other year. Some adult birds may spend up to five years at sea between breeding seasons. Young albatrosses can spend up to six years away from land, gliding over the Southern Ocean, until the desire for a mate draws them back to their birthplace for their first breeding attempt. It can be a further four years before they start breeding successfully. Many of the smaller seabirds are five years old before they reach breeding age.

Most seabirds return to their island of origin, many to the same colony. This phenomenon has led to many species of mollymawks (small albatrosses) being

Left: Pair of Buller's mollymawks
ANDRIS APSE

Below: Royal albatrosses
CAROL WEST

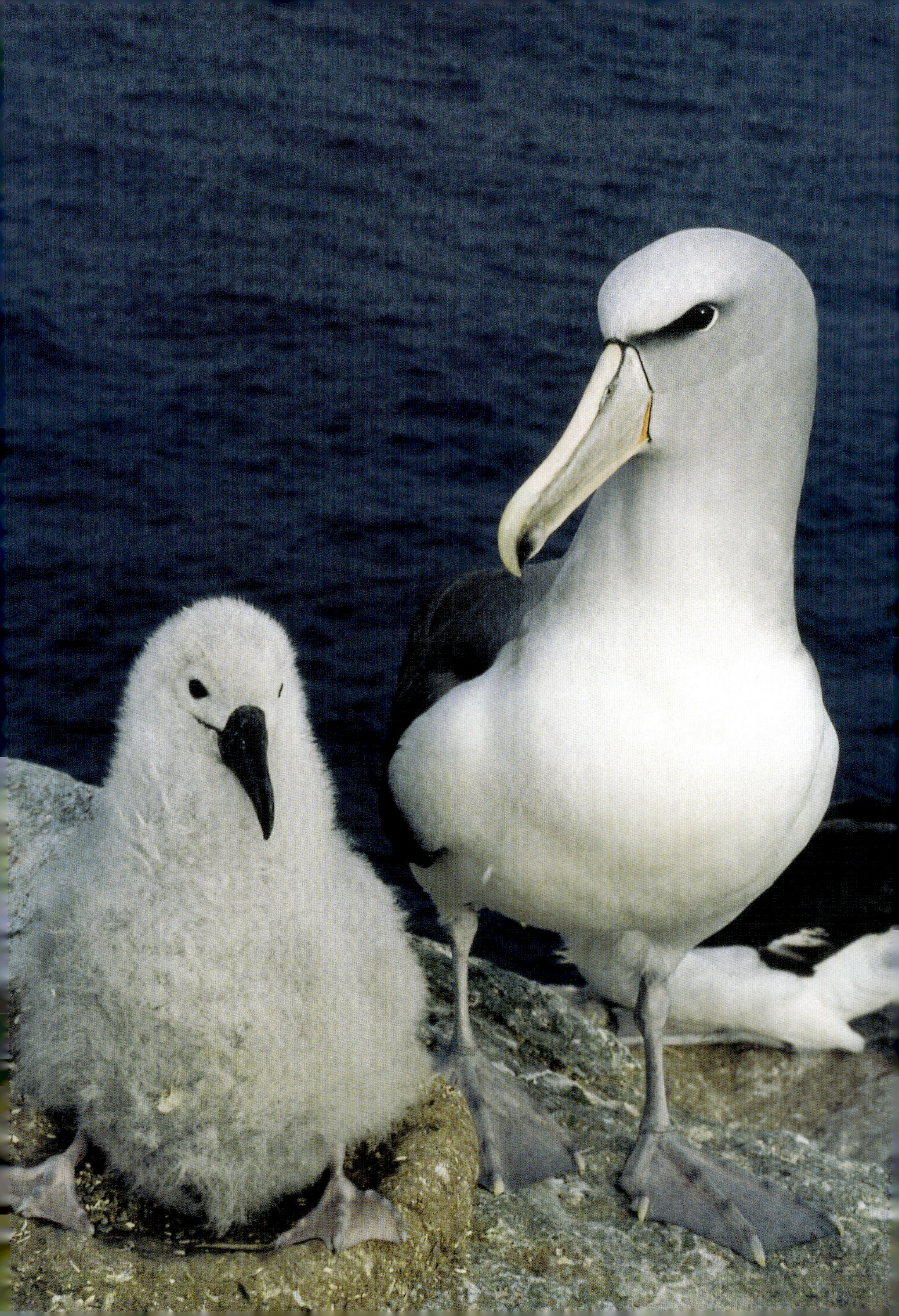

found only on one of the island groups. However, some species will sometimes colonise new areas. One example of this is the small population of royal albatrosses which breed on Enderby Island. This population was wiped out during the sealing and castaway era, but has now re-established and numbers are slowly building.

The seabirds which breed on these islands range in size from delicate storm petrels, which will fit into a human hand, to the great albatrosses, with wing spans in excess of 3.3 metres.

New Zealand is one of the countries which distinguishes between the larger albatrosses (royal and wandering albatross) and their smaller cousins, the mollymawks. These are the birds which most frequently follow boats in subantarctic waters. Their size and effortless grace in the air makes them the most obvious and easily recognised of the seabirds.

Eleven species of this extended family of seabirds breed on New Zealand's subantarctic islands, six on Campbell alone, a diversity exceeded only on the Crozet Islands in the southern Indian Ocean. Recent research using satellite tracking has shown that some albatrosses will travel many thousands of kilometres in a single feeding trip.

An example of this is Gibson's albatross. Breeding birds frequently fly from their breeding colonies on Adams Island to the south coast of Australia and back. They can cover up to 1000 km a day on these epic flights, returning to feed a chick and relieve brooding mates on the nest.

Their surface nesting behaviour and extraordinary tameness make albatrosses easy to observe and study. This contrasts with the burrow nests of many smaller species of petrel, shearwater, prion, storm petrel and diving petrel, which make studies or even accurate counts of these species very difficult. Most of the eighteen or so smaller petrels belong to species which are widely distributed in the Southern Ocean. The most notable exception is the mottled petrel, which breeds only on The Snares and islands off Stewart Island and Fiordland.

Opposite: Salvin's mollymawk and chick
ANDREA BOOTH

Grey-headed mollymawk
GREG LIND

Light-mantled Sooty albatrosses
Lou Sanson

Most of the petrels return to the islands after dark and leave before dawn to avoid the attention of predatory southern skuas. A vast population of sooty shearwaters, estimated at nearly three million pairs, nests on The Snares. Congregating offshore well before dark, they descend on their burrows in their thousands, forming one of nature's great sights. At dawn they leave the islands like a black cloud, taking off from any suitable clifftop runway.

Although dependent on the land during the breeding season, all of these birds rely on the sea for food. When feeding chicks it is not unusual for adults to spend over five days at sea, harvesting the rich waters surrounding the islands. While the petrels search the ocean for food from above, penguins are searching from below.

Ten species of penguin have been recorded on New Zealand's subantarctic islands, and four of these regularly breed there. They include the solitary nesting yellow-eyed penguins, which come ashore in the late afternoon at breeding sites on Auckland and Campbell Islands. In contrast, the other three species, which are all crested penguins, form large colonies. The Snares crested penguin is found only on the island group from which it takes its name. Erect-crested penguins are now confined to the Bounty and Antipodes Islands, while the

Above: Wandering albatrosses
Lou Sanson

Below: New Zealand black-browed mollymawks
Carol West

Yellow-eyed penguin
CHRIS RANCE

smaller rockhopper penguin breeds on Antipodes, Auckland and Campbell Islands, as well as on other islands in the Southern Ocean. Crested penguins breed and moult ashore then leave their breeding islands for about four months during the winter. Where they go is yet to be discovered.

In recent years there has been a dramatic decline in the number of erect-crested and rockhopper penguins. Numbers of rockhopper penguins have fallen by about 90 percent in 50 years on Campbell Island, and there has been an estimated 20 percent decline in erect-crested penguin numbers on the Antipodes Islands since the mid-1990s. The reason for this is yet to be confirmed; it may relate to changes affecting the birds at sea. An increase in ocean temperatures, which pushes food species further south into colder waters, is a possible cause of the decline.

Like the yellow-eyed penguin, the various marine shags (cormorants) feed at sea but return to land each night to roost, and are present on the islands throughout the year. Each of the three species found in the area is endemic to its own island group, namely the Auckland, Campbell and Bounty Island shags. The Bounty Island shag is considered one of the world's rarest

Snares crested penguin and chick
BRIAN RANCE

cormorants, with a population of fewer than 600 individuals.

Gulls, terns and skua are present on all islands, but the species composition varies from group to group. The southern skua fills the role of both predator and scavenger in the subantarctic. They eat carrion, kill seabirds — including many larger than themselves — and take penguin eggs and chicks. They are present on all islands except the Bounties, where the density of other seabirds prevents them from finding enough space to build a nest.

Southern black-backed gulls, also known as kelp or Dominican gulls, are also widespread, although they are rare stragglers to The Snares. Red-billed or silver gulls are absent from the Bounty and Antipodes Islands. Dainty but noisy Antarctic terns breed in small numbers on all of the island groups, and the larger white-fronted tern also occurs on the Auckland Islands.

Erect-crested penguin
ANDREA BOOTH

Rockhopper penguins
Wynston Cooper

Opposite: Campbell Island shags
Carol West

Giant petrels are one of the most distinctive of the subantarctic seabirds. These large grey birds, also known as nellies or stinkers from their chicks' defensive habit of spewing foul-smelling stomach contents at intruders, frequently join albatrosses as they follow boats looking for scraps.

The diversity of land-birds and freshwater birds on each island is largely determined by the size of the island and the range of habitats available. Some mainland New Zealand species reach their southern limit at The Snares. Climate and isolation also play a role in determining which species become established. The Auckland Islands have the greatest diversity of native land-birds, with over thirteen species, including the New Zealand falcon and two species of honey-eater (tui and bellbird). In contrast, the barren Bounty Islands and the Western Chain islets of The Snares have no land-birds.

Some native New Zealand bird species have survived on the subantarctic islands long after they were exterminated by introduced predators on the mainland. New Zealand snipe thrive on The Snares, Antipodes Island and on some islands in the Auckland Island group, which have remained free of cats and pigs. Although numerous, these relatively tame birds are rarely seen owing to the dense vegetation that they inhabit. This was shown by the discovery of snipe on one of the small islands off Campbell Island in 1997, the first time they had been recorded on the group. Even more secretive is the Auckland Island rail, recently rediscovered on predator-free Adams and Disappointment Islands.

Many land-birds have evolved into distinctive forms endemic to one island group. Eleven subspecies and three full species are currently recognised as being endemic to

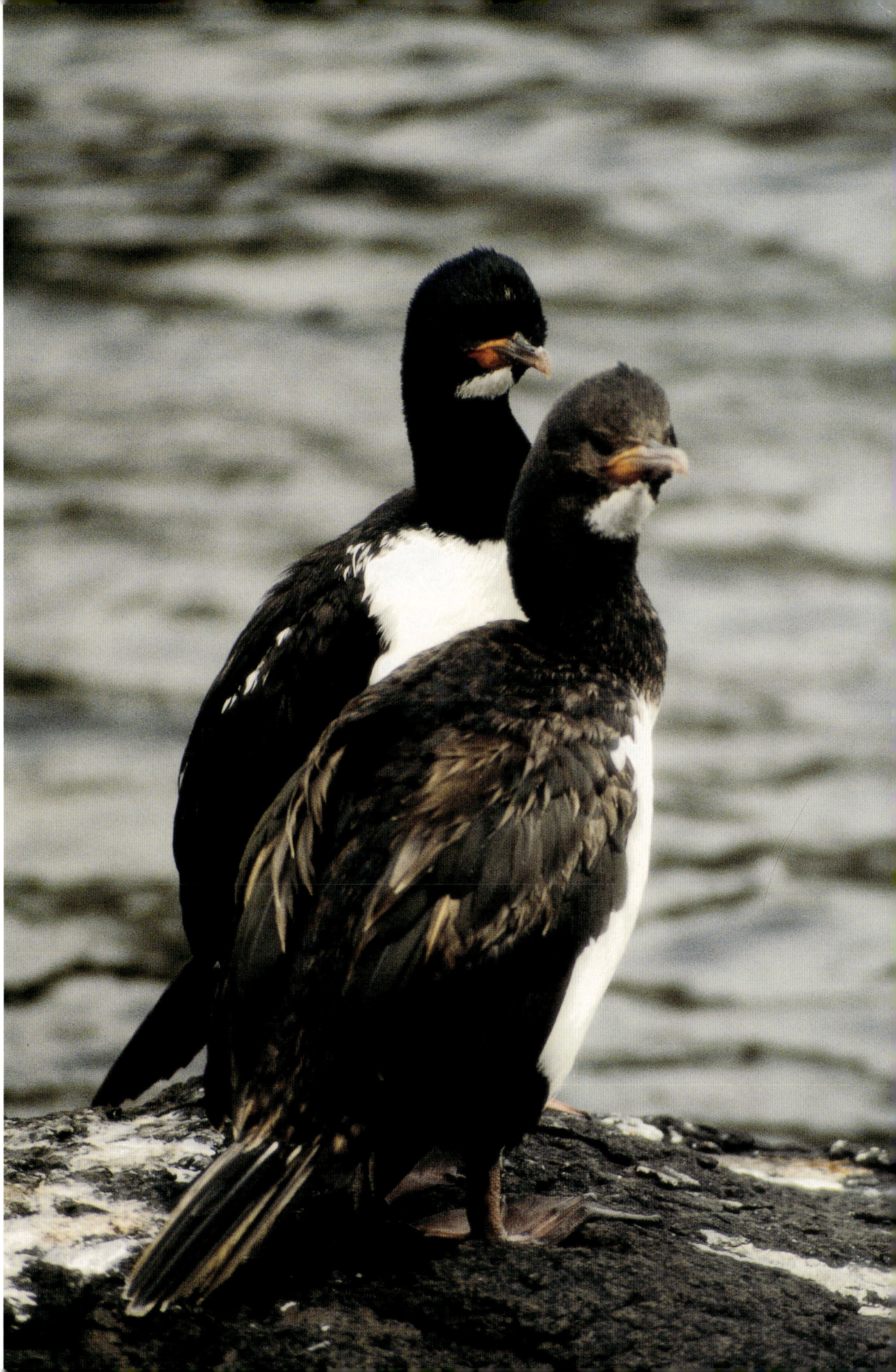

Above: Southern skua
Chris Rance

Below: Giant petrel
Carol West

Right: New Zealand falcon
Lou Sanson

have independently evolved into flightless forms. Recent genetic evidence suggests these birds have undergone parallel evolution from separate invasions of brown teal from New Zealand, with the Auckland Island teal becoming established after the Campbell Island population.

Flightlessness is a feature of the New Zealand avifauna, but it is not particularly prevalent among subantarctic birds. However, several other forms, including the four snipe, the Auckland Island rail and Snares fernbird, have reduced powers of flight.

The characteristic tameness of subantarctic land-birds, combined with their ground-nesting habit and unwillingness to fly, has made them vulnerable to introduced mammalian predators. This problem has, in some cases, been accentuated by the presence of introduced herbivores which, over

islands in the New Zealand subantarctic region. The Auckland Islands have the highest number of endemic birds, with a teal, a rail, a plover, a snipe, a dotterel, a pipit and a tomtit. All four native Antipodes Island land-birds are endemic — two parakeets, a snipe and a pipit. The Snares have three endemic birds — a snipe, a fernbird and a tomtit. Campbell Island has a pipit, an endemic teal now confined to outlying Dent Island, and a snipe that is also confined to one small offshore island.

The small teals of Auckland and Campbell Islands are of particular interest as they

Above: Bellbird
PETE McCLELLAND

Below: Auckland Island snipe
LOU SANSON

the past 150 years, have drastically altered the vegetation on some islands, reducing cover for many species. The fact that some islands in each group remain free of introduced predators has been vital for the survival of some endemic land-birds.

The tomtits on The Snares and Auckland Islands have evolved in quite separate ways from their presumed mainland New Zealand ancestor. Tomtits on the mainland are sexually dimorphic, with pied males and drab brown/grey females. On the Auckland Islands the females closely resemble males, with black heads and white and yellow underparts. On The Snares both sexes are completely black, and for many years naturalists confused them with the larger, and much rarer, black robin of the Chatham Islands.

Two species of parakeet occur on both Auckland Island and Antipodes Island. On the Auckland Islands the red-crowned and yellow-crowned parakeets are considered identical with mainland New Zealand forms. As on the mainland, the two forms maintain distinct niches; red-crowned parakeets favouring open, low vegetation and yellow-crowned parakeets preferring more upright scrub and forest. The parakeets on the Antipodes are both endemic forms, and are thought to have evolved following a

Above: Auckland Island pipit
PETE MCCLELLAND

Right: Auckland Island teal
PETE MCCLELLAND

double invasion of a similar ancestor. The Antipodes Island parakeet is presumed to be the original colonist and has evolved into a separate species. This bird is larger than the other parakeets and has lost its coloured crown, whereas the smaller Reischek's parakeet is similar in appearance to the red-crowned parakeet. It is remarkable that two endemic parakeets could evolve on an island of only 2000 ha, but the two forms are ecologically and morphologically distinct. Until recently it was thought the Antipodes Island parakeets fed mainly on leaves of tussock and sedge, while Reischek's parakeets were predominantly seed-eaters. However, the Antipodes Island parakeet has been observed scavenging dead seabirds and was recently recorded killing grey-backed storm petrels in their tussock burrows.

All the land-birds are presumed to have flown, or been blown, to the islands from mainland New Zealand or Australia, and this process is continuing. Between 1977 and 1982 South Island fantails colonised The Snares, presumably from Stewart Island, and now have a large, breeding population there. Over the last 120 years many species of birds have been introduced to mainland New Zealand by humans, and at least ten species have successfully colonised one or more subantarctic island group. Species that have managed to colonise three or more groups include the mallard, song thrush, blackbird, chaffinch, goldfinch, redpoll and starling.

Many other species have reached various subantarctic islands as vagrants, but have failed to establish breeding populations.

Parakeet, Ewing Island, Auckland Islands
PETE MCCLELLAND

Auckland Island banded dotterel
Greg Lind

The list includes Asiatic migrants which have overflown the mark, such as various waders, swifts and cuckoos, as well as stray New Zealand and Australian species such as grebes, cormorants, egrets, waterfowl, harriers, gallinules, waders, pigeons, parakeets, cuckoos, owls and a wide range of passerines. Some migrant waders, especially turnstones, reach the Auckland Islands every year, where they forage with endemic Auckland Island banded dotterels on Enderby Island. There is little habitat suitable for waders on the other islands.

Regardless of the primary reason for visiting the New Zealand subantarctic, the abundance, variety and tameness of the birds on the islands and at sea proves a highlight of any trip.

Freshwater Fauna

The freshwater communities of the subantarctic islands are often overlooked and few people appreciate the variety of life in the streams, rivers, ponds and lakes of these islands.

Various invertebrates and one fish species have been recorded from the freshwater communities of the subantarctic islands. The greatest diversity of invertebrates is present on the Auckland and Campbell Islands, reflecting their larger land areas and wider variety of permanent freshwater habitats. The Auckland Islands contain the highest number of species, probably as a result of their closer proximity to mainland New Zealand. On Antipodes and Snares Islands freshwater habitats are limited. Many are ephemeral or heavily polluted by seabird excrement, and few freshwater species have been recorded. There are no permanent freshwater habitats on the Bounty Islands.

Stream, Kekeno Point, Auckland Island
PETE MCCLELLAND

Streams are typically a deep reddish-brown colour, which is created by dissolved organic material from the peaty soils and breakdown of leaf matter. Water chemistry is strongly influenced by the oceanic climate, with a high ionic content dominated by windblown sea salts. Streams are often moderately acidic, a natural feature of the water chemistry, as is the characteristic foam sometimes observed on the surface of pools which also runs beneath small cascades or rapids.

Freshwater insects are predominantly cool-adapted species and the number on the islands is low compared with mainland New Zealand. There is a high degree of endemism, with many species representing genera not found on the mainland (see table). The stoneflies (Plecoptera), for example, show a close affinity with mainland species but, owing to their long isolation, are all unique species; the genus *Aucklandobius* is recorded only on the Auckland Islands, *Rungaperla* only on Campbell Island, and *Nesoperla johnsi* on The Snares. A single species of mayfly, a dominant group of aquatic invertebrates on the mainland, has been recorded on the Auckland Islands. The Auckland Islands are the southernmost limit of mayflies (Ephemeroptera) in New Zealand. The caddis flies (Trichoptera) are a mixture of endemics and a cosmopolitan species. The purse caddis *Oxyethira albiceps* is present on Campbell, Auckland and the Antipodes Islands and The Snares as well as mainland New Zealand and the Chatham

Koaro
G.A. Eldon

Islands. Two species of *Hydrobiosidae* are endemic to the Auckland Islands.

The largest and most conspicuous invertebrates are the stoneflies and the freshwater slater *Notidotea lacustris* (Crustacea). Both can be found beneath stones or within leaf-packs and are between 10 and 20 mm long. Stoneflies are surface browsers, feeding on the organic film on rocks. The slater is more precisely a freshwater isopod and a relative of the common woodlouse. It is probably omnivorous, feeding on other stream invertebrates as well as leaf and woody material, and is the dominant invertebrate in most Campbell Island streams. It appears to be more widespread than similar species found on the New Zealand mainland.

Many of the aquatic insects present are larval life history stages which emerge from streams as terrestrial winged adults. Stoneflies, caddisflies, the mayfly and various true flies or Diptera, like the midges and craneflies, all have a terrestrial adult lifestage. Perhaps the best known example is the common sandfly, of which the female is the annoying bloodsucker. The sandfly is actually a blackfly or simuliid, and its larvae are small aquatic filter feeders which trap fine food particles, including bacteria, from the water column.

	Snares	Auckland	Campbell	Antipodes
Ephemeroptera		1		
Plecoptera	1	2	1	
Trichoptera		2		
Diptera		12	7	3
Crustacea		1	1	
Mollusca		1		
Total	1	19	9	3

Numbers of endemic freshwater invertebrate species known to be present only on the subantarctic islands.

Stream, North Harbour, Auckland Island
WYNSTON COOPER

Freshwater fish

Koaro or *Galaxias brevipinnis* is the only freshwater fish recorded in the subantarctic islands. It commonly grows to a length of 160–180 mm, lacks scales and has a single dorsal fin. This galaxiid is an Australasian species and belongs to an ancient family of fishes of Gondwanan origin. It is present on both Campbell and Auckland Islands and is widespread on the main islands of New Zealand, Tasmania and South Australia.

In the subantarctic islands adult fish are resident in freshwater, whereas young larvae are flushed out to sea once they hatch, returning to freshwater as small transparent juvenile fish. The young fish are very agile climbers, capable of negotiating waterfalls many metres high. Hence, these fish can be found well inland on both subantarctic island groups. They are active during the day and occupy a wide range of habitats including pools and backwaters as well as the rapid-flowing, tumbling, rocky reaches from which koaro are more commonly known on the mainland. Although a cryptic or well-camouflaged species, the patient observer should see these golden brown fish in pools of coastal streams.

Teal Lake, Enderby Island, Auckland Islands
CHRIS RANCE

SEALS AND WHALES

Seals

Of the four species of seals which regularly visit New Zealand's subantarctic islands one is endemic (found nowhere else), one is found around New Zealand and in Australia, and two are common throughout the Southern Ocean.

The New Zealand (Hooker's) sea lion and New Zealand fur seal are otariids, or eared seals. They have external ears, and can turn their hind flippers forward to walk on all fours. Otariids primarily use their front flippers for power when swimming. Fur seals can be distinguished by their thick, dense underfur which insulates them from the cold, formerly highly prized by early sealers.

New Zealand (Hooker's) sea lion, male
CAROL WEST

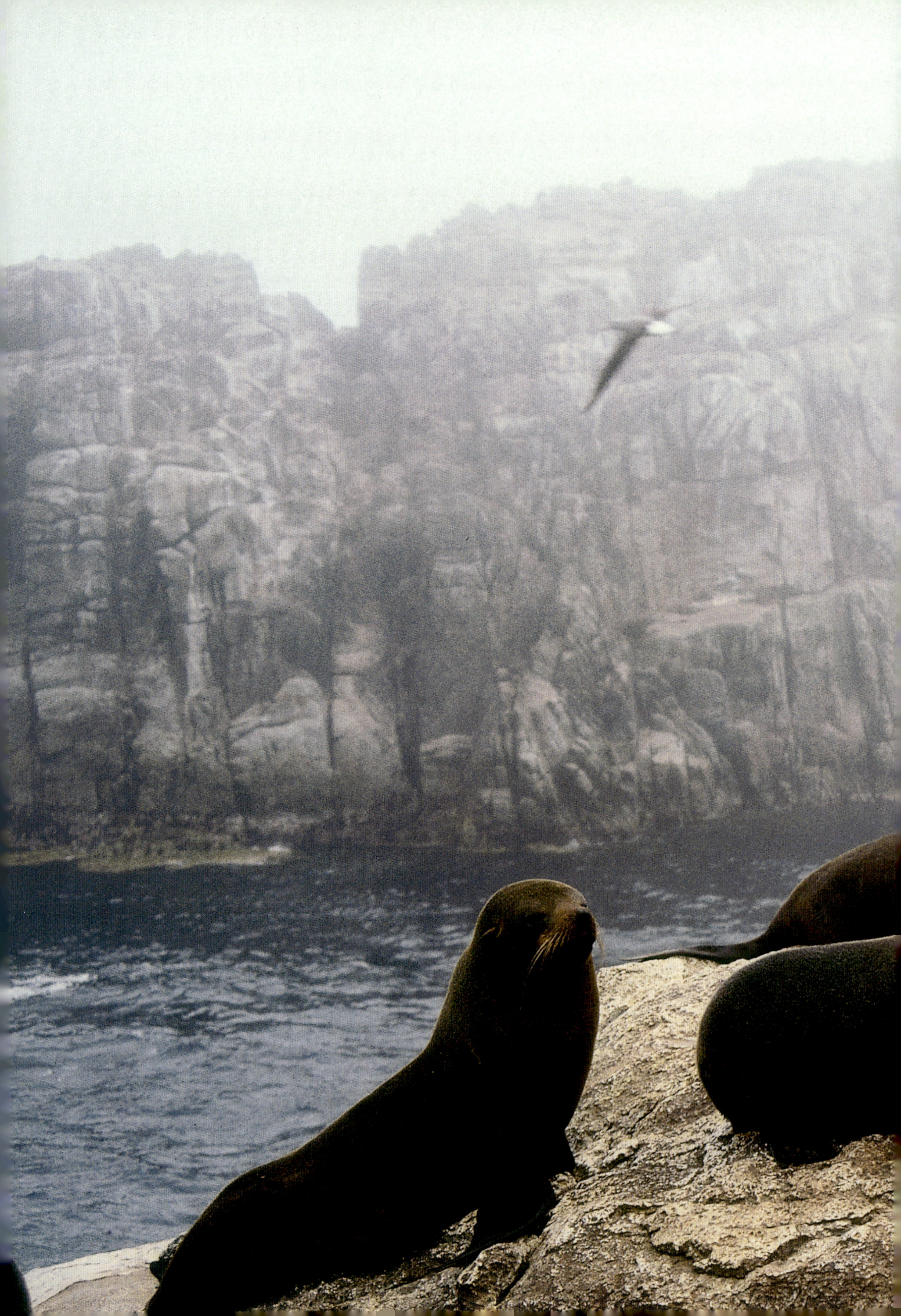

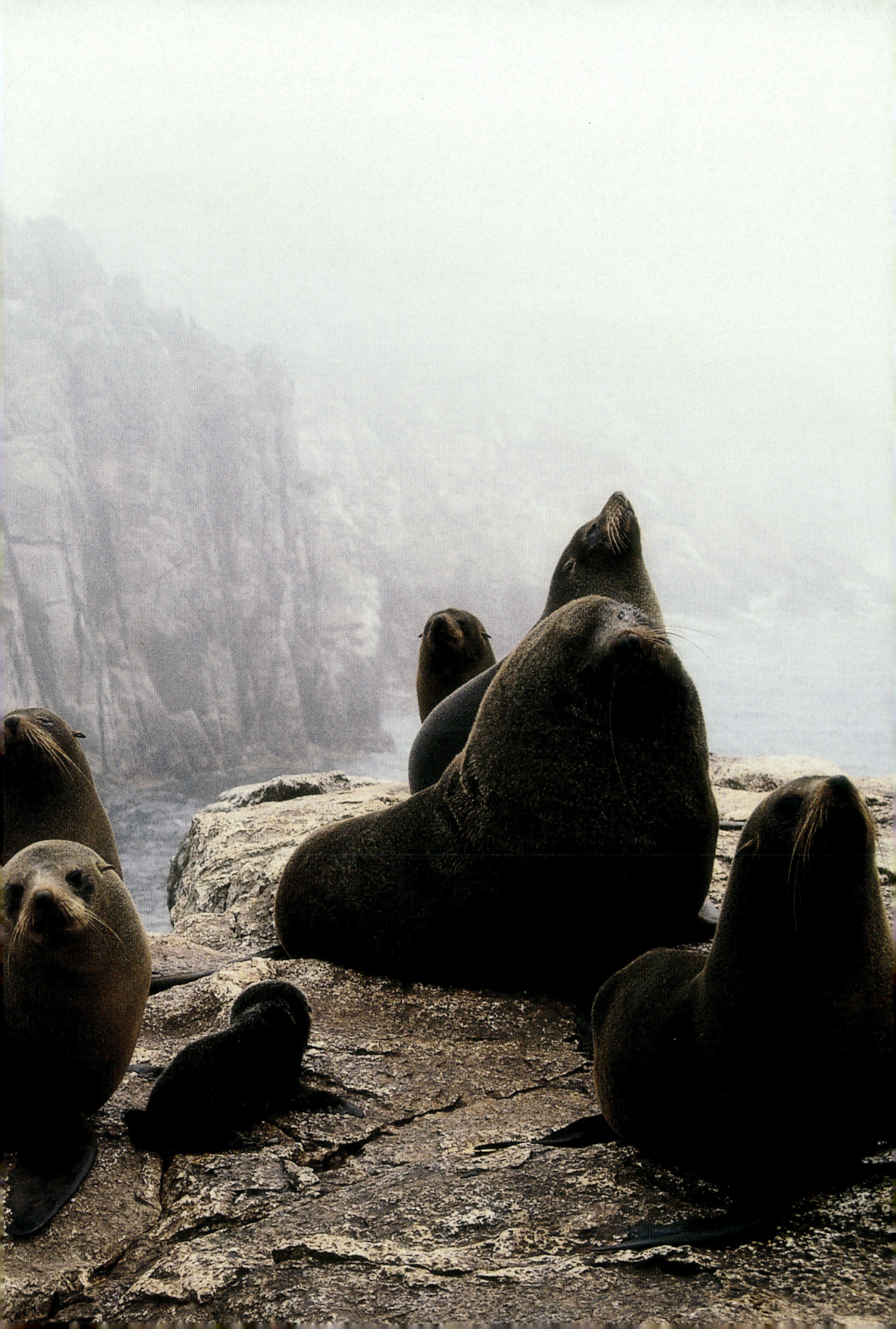

Previous page: New Zealand fur seals
GREG LIND

The other two species, the southern elephant seal and the leopard seal, are phocids or true seals. They do not have external ears and cannot swing their hind flippers forward as they are fused together and create the driving force when swimming. These seals progress on land by hitching along, caterpillar fashion and, rather than having thick fur, are insulated by a subcutaneous layer of fat or blubber. Crabeater and Weddell seals, which are also phocids and normally restricted to the Antarctic pack ice, occasionally turn up on the subantarctic islands.

All seals in New Zealand are protected under the Marine Mammals Protection Act 1978. They are powerful, and potentially dangerous, wild animals and should be approached cautiously and no closer than 10 metres. Even the smallest seal can inflict serious injury if it is cornered or feels threatened.

New Zealand fur seals

New Zealand fur seals (*Arctocephalus forsteri*) are common around the New Zealand mainland, on offshore islands, and on the south coast of Australia. They were hunted by early Maori and almost exterminated by European sealers during the eighteenth and nineteenth centuries.

Fur seals were first taken commercially in 1792; by 1815 the boom years were over. In one season a single vessel took about 60,000 skins from the Antipodes Islands alone. This is more than estimates of the entire New Zealand fur seal population today. Hunting was closed in 1894, although licences were issued sporadically in 1913, 1916, 1922–24, and for the last time in 1946 when fishermen who believed that seals were depleting local fish stocks were permitted a cull. Today the population is increasing and recolonising much of its former range throughout New Zealand.

The current New Zealand population is estimated at about 50,000, with most occurring on the west and south coasts of the South Island and on subantarctic islands. The Bounty Islands are home to the largest concentrations in New Zealand, with an estimated 21,500 recorded in 1994. There are estimated to be approximately 35,000 in Australia. Some colonies on the New Zealand mainland are increasing at rates of over 10 percent per annum.

New Zealand fur seals are generally found on rocky outcrops or platforms. Males assemble at breeding colonies in October and contest for territories where they establish harems. The females arrive about a month later and their pups are born two to three days after they come ashore. Pupping continues through to late December, with most born around December 9–10.

Females suckle pups for about 300 days, making regular feeding trips to sea during the season, each trip lasting between one and five days. Pups grow rapidly and gain between 45 and 75 grams per day while suckling. Adult males weigh between 120 and 180 kg, and reach between 1.5 and 2.5 metres in length. Adult females are considerably smaller and lighter, weighing between 30 and 50 kg, and reaching up to 70 cm in length.

New Zealand fur seals are opportunistic feeders with a preference for octopus, squid and some inshore fish species including lanternfish and hoki. Females have been recorded diving to 270 metres while searching for food. Some individuals are accidentally caught in fishing operations each year.

New Zealand (Hooker's) sea lions

The New Zealand, or Hooker's, sea lion (*Phocarctos hookeri*) is one of the rarest of the five species of sea lion in the world. It is listed as threatened by the International Union for the Conservation of Nature and protected by New Zealand legislation.

In pre-European times sea lions ranged the length of New Zealand and were taken by Maori as a source of food. They are thought to have been hunted to extinction on the mainland soon after European arrival in the 1770s. They have survived as remnant populations in the New Zealand subantarctic.

Unlike fur seals, which were exploited only for their pelts, sea lions were also taken for oils rendered from their thick, insulating blubber. The sealers and whalers were particularly efficient. By 1829 the sea lion population had been reduced to such a low level that when Captain Morrell visited the Auckland Islands in late December, the time of the present breeding season, he found no fur seals and only five sea lions.

The present range of the species is confined to a triangle bounded by the southern South Island, Campbell Island and Macquarie Island, and the population was estimated to be between 12,800 and 17,200 in January 1998. The population is centred on the Auckland Islands where 95 percent of the animals breed in three major colonies. There is also some breeding on Campbell Island with a few individuals breeding on mainland New Zealand.

New Zealand (Hooker's) sea lion, female.
CHRIS RANCE

New Zealand sea lions
Carol West

One of the major threats facing the sea lion population is the impact of squid trawlers working around the islands, which accidentally catch and drown an estimated 70–100 sea lions in their nets each year. The commercial squid fishery uses a number of methods to avoid these deaths and is closed for the season when the sea lion bycatch reaches a preset number. In January 1998 an unidentified illness during the breeding season killed at least 1700 sea lions on their main breeding beaches. More than 53 percent of the pups born that year and perhaps 20 percent of adults died during the summer breeding season. The impact of this level of mortality on the population will not be clear for several years, but it is likely to have had a significant effect on the recovery of the species.

Sea lions congregate at the colonies for two and a half months each year. Males arrive in late November and take up beach territories, which they hold until late January. The females start arriving in the first week of December and pup about seven days after arrival. Mating follows seven to ten days after pupping. By mid-January breeding has finished and the dominant bulls begin to disperse from the colonies.

After males have left the colonies females take their pups to safe places around the island, sometimes several kilometres inland, where they leave them while they make foraging trips to offshore feeding grounds. Females feed up to 140 km offshore on the edge of the Auckland Islands shelf, where they generally hunt in waters between 100 and 200 metres deep, although they can dive to 570 metres. They can be away from their pups from two to five days. They are opportunistic feeders and take octopus, squid, rattails and hoki. They will also occasionally kill and eat penguins and fur seals.

Adult male sea lions grow to at least 450 kg and can be over 3 metres in length. The females reach 160 kg and are 2 metres in length. Pups weigh about 8 to 10 kg at birth. Females reach sexual maturity at about four years and may produce one pup annually. Males are physically mature at about five years, but generally do not hold a territory in the colony until they are at least nine or ten years old.

Southern elephant seals

Southern elephant seals (*Mirounga leonina*), which were once common throughout the Southern Ocean, were also heavily exploited for their oil until the turn of the twentieth century. They are the largest of all pinniped (having feet which resemble fins) mammals of the order Carnivora, with adult males averaging 2.2 tonnes and a length of 4.2 metres, but they can reach 5 tonnes and 6.2 metres. Females are significantly smaller at 500 kg and 2.7 metres in length.

The elephant seal is a circumpolar species with colonies throughout the subantarctic. Three separate stocks are recognised; one centred on South Georgia, one at Iles

Kerguelen, and the third centred on Macquarie Island and including New Zealand's subantarctic islands.

The New Zealand breeding colonies are restricted to Campbell and Antipodes Islands. Although the Macquarie stock of elephant seals has been free from human exploitation for close to a century, Australian researchers report a 50 percent decrease in the population since 1949. Breeding on Campbell Island has also declined dramatically, by over 90 percent over the last 40 years, to less than 20 pups a year. No reliable data on the Antipodes Island population is available but it appears to be stable.

As a top predator, elephant seals are valuable as an indicator species, and trends shown by their populations may reflect the general health of the Southern Ocean ecosystem. Populations appear to be declining throughout the southern hemisphere, for reasons that are as yet unclear.

Southern elephant seal
CRAIG POTTON

New Zealand's Subantarctic Islands

Southern elephant seals
Carol West

Breeding takes place from September to October in the New Zealand subantarctic and mating follows about three weeks after pups are born. Mature males come ashore to establish their territories two weeks before the females, in mid-August. Large males, often scarred from battles for territory, attract harems of females.

Elephant seals spend all their time at sea outside the breeding and moulting periods and roam widely. They range as far north as the North Island of New Zealand, and two females have had pups on remote beaches in Otago.

Elephant seals are the champion divers among seals, having been recorded descending more than 1200 metres in search of prey.

Leopard seals

Leopard seals (*Hydrurga leptonyx*) are regular visitors to all the New Zealand subantarctic islands, but they are usually found further south on the edges of the Antarctic pack ice. They have large, sleek, serpentine heads with sharp pointed teeth, and streamlined bodies with mottled markings.

Leopard seals mate at sea and do not form colonies, therefore little is known about their breeding cycle.

Adult males weigh between 200 and 455 kg and measure between 2.5 and 3.2 metres

Leopard seal
Lou Sanson

in length, while females are slightly larger at 225 to 590 kg and between 2.4 and 3.4 metres in length.

Krill is an important part of their diet in winter but they also feed on squid and fish. They are the only seal that regularly eats warm-blooded prey, such as penguins and fur seals.

Whales

New Zealand and its subantarctic islands straddle the north–south migratory routes between the Antarctic feeding areas and tropical/temperate breeding grounds of many whales found in the South Pacific Ocean.

The baleen whales — the fin, sei, right, blue and humpback whales — are sometimes seen around the New Zealand subantarctic islands. Sperm, pilot and beaked whales, all toothed whales, are also occasionally seen in the area.

Two baleen whales, the humpback and southern right, were the primary targets of the New Zealand whaling industry during the nineteenth century. The harvest of whales was so extensive that the slow-moving southern right whale was virtually exterminated by the 1840s. It is probable that the few southern right whales which mated and calved at Campbell Island saved this species from extinction in the New Zealand area. The total population of southern right whales in New Zealand and eastern Australia is still estimated at fewer than 1000 animals. Around 200 years ago, at the start of the whaling era, the population was estimated at about 60,000 whales.

A breeding population of at least 100 southern right whales gathers in Port Ross in the Auckland Islands between June and September each year. Cow and calf pairs are commonly found in the sheltered waters of the bays, inlets and harbours, and active groups of mating adults can also be seen. There is also a small group of whales which visits Northwest Bay in Campbell Island each year. Boats which encounter whales should move slowly around them and keep at least 100 metres away to avoid disturbing them.

Three small cetaceans — the hourglass and dusky dolphin and the spectacled porpoise — are restricted to these latitudes and are occasionally seen. The slightly larger southern right whale dolphin, with its distinctive black and white coloration and lack of a dorsal fin, can sometimes be seen in the New Zealand subantarctic. Orca, or killer whales, are occasional visitors and are one of the principal predators of seals and small whales in the region.

Southern right whale
ANDRIS APSE

Marine Life

Although the islands are popularly called 'subantarctic', and are surrounded by so-called subantarctic water, their nearshore marine biota is not truly subantarctic.

Sea surface temperatures in the region range from a summer monthly mean of 12°C at The Snares to a winter monthly mean of 5.5° C at Campbell Island. Therefore, the marine biota is more appropriately described as cool temperate.

Because the islands are so widely separated and are of widely different geological ages, it is difficult to generalise about their marine life. Each island has its own unique assemblage of seaweeds, invertebrates and fish, although for each island the marine biota comprises three groups. The largest is made up of species that are also found, or have close relatives, on the New Zealand mainland. A smaller group comprises circum-subantarctic species, and in

Starfish attacking yellowfoot paua
PETE MCCLELLAND

Durvillaea antarctica
ANDREA BOOTH

addition each island supports a small endemic element.

One feature that is common to all the islands is the relatively low diversity of seaweeds and (especially) animals when compared with the New Zealand mainland. For the marine biologist, much of the fascination of these islands is not in noting the species one might expect to find, but noting those which are absent.

Absent are many of the common New Zealand brown seaweeds like Neptune's necklace (*Hormosira banksii*), *Durvillaea willana*, *Ecklonia radiata* and *Carpophyllum* spp.; green seaweeds such as species of *Caulerpa*; and a variety of red algae. Some reach their southern limit at The Snares.

The same applies to many common marine mainland animals, including some of the most desirable edible species — crayfish, paua, scallops, blue cod, blue moki and tarakihi — which also reach their southern limit at The Snares. At the other islands fishers will soon find their catch confined to three very similar species of black cod (or Maori chief); *Notothenia microlepidota*, *N. angustata* and *N. magellanica*. Although they are easily hooked, the flesh of these fish is often infested with large parasitic worms.

The most conspicuous seaweed on all of the islands is the massive bull-kelp (*Durvillaea antarctica*), which forms a thick kelp band just above the low watermark; it grows both in sheltered locations and on headlands with strong wave action. This amazing plant, with its huge, sucker-like holdfasts, stout, rubbery stalks and buoyant, honeycombed blades weighing more than 50 kg, girdles all of New Zealand's southern islands, and much of the mainland coast.

Where wave action is slightly reduced, the brown alga *Xiphophora gladiata* grows abundantly. This leathery, dichotomously branching plant, rarely longer than 50 cm, is found on all islands, and is particularly abundant within the harbours of Auckland and Campbell Islands.

The giant kelp *Macrocystis pyrifera* forms extensive beds inside the harbours of Auckland and Campbell Islands, its golden blades and bladders floating at the surface.

In the intertidal zone are species of red algae, including slippery beds of *Porphyra* spp. such as *P. columbina*, which frequently make walking difficult for visitors to the islands.

Common intertidal animals vary from island to island. At Auckland and Campbell Islands there is a low intertidal band of blue mussel (*Mytilus galloprovincialis*) and ribbed mussel (*Aulacomya atra maoriana*), while the Antipodes have no mussels in the intertidal or shallow subtidal regions.

Within the intertidal zone limpets are important on all the islands. Chitons, however, are relatively sparse. The subantarctic whelk genus *Pareuthria* is represented on Campbell and Antipodes Islands, while zone-forming barnacles — common on the mainland — appear relatively uncommon on the islands.

Subtidally, immediately below the zone of kelp, much of the rock surface is covered with calcareous red algae, particularly encrusting forms.

The brown kelp *Lessonia brevifolia* is abundant on open coasts to a depth of 30 metres. At Antipodes Island a massive, undescribed species of *Durvillaea* forms a wide subtidal band. Encrusting sponges and tunicates are scarce, possibly because they are unable to compete with the algae, particularly the calcareous forms.

On all the islands the largest mollusc in the subtidal zone is the brown mussel, *Modiolus areolatus*. The crab *Jacquinotia edwardsi* is the largest crustacean, with a

Limpet eggs
PETE MCCLELLAND

carapace that is over 150 mm wide; it is exceedingly abundant around Auckland and Campbell Islands.

Much more baseline information about the marine flora and fauna and its ecology is needed before scientists can attempt to understand how the various animals and seaweeds interact on these southern islands. The rather low diversity of large invertebrates and fish suggests that selective harvesting of any one species could have major ecological implications, particularly on the smaller islands.

Seaweeds at Snares Islands
Carol West

INTRODUCED SPECIES

Oceanic islands are among the last bastions of nature in a world beset by massive and rapid change through human activity. New Zealand's subantarctic islands are some of the least human-modified environments anywhere in the world. Maintenance of these island ecosystems in their natural state is of immense value to global conservation and science. Experience has shown that plants and animals which have evolved on oceanic islands in the absence of terrestrial mammals are highly vulnerable and sensitive to disturbance. They are easily destroyed and usually impossible to replace.

The colonisation of an island by a new species will result in permanent change. The extent of the change may be relatively benign or it may be absolutely devastating, as was the case when rats reached Big South Cape Island off the southwest coast of Stewart Island in the

Cattle and yellow-eyed penguins on Enderby Island
PETE MCCLELLAND

1960s. Two species of native birds and the native greater short-tailed bat became extinct. Many other species survive in much reduced numbers.

The highest priority for island conservation is to prevent the establishment of new species, and it is essential that all visitors implement quarantine measures to prevent species reaching the islands. While the greatest emphasis is on species most likely to be transported, and those which will do the most damage, quarantine measures must protect the islands against the full range of potential invaders. These include plants, pathogens and all animals from invertebrates to mammals. Contingency plans and equipment must be ready to prevent a population of alien species becoming established if quarantine is unsuccessful. In the past, populations of introduced animals have become established as a result of a lack of quarantine, attempts to establish farming, or to supply food for castaways.

Among the islands, only Campbell and Auckland Islands have considerable numbers of alien plants (85 species and 37 species respectively), but fortunately none of them poses a threat to indigenous vegetation at present. Usually, introduced plants have been successful only on artificially disturbed ground, and they eventually succumb to competition from indigenous plants. Of the two introduced plants on The Snares, one, chickweed (*Stellaria media*), is being eradicated, while the other, annual poa (*Poa annua*), is much too widespread to control.

The Snares, Bounties and most offshore islands in other groups are without introduced mammals of any kind, and the Antipodes has only the house mouse. The Auckland group has pigs, cats and mice, while Campbell Island has Norway rats. A comprehensive approach to alien mammal control within the island groups is being developed.

To allow island habitats and species to recover, a number of introduced populations have been eradicated. These include sheep from Campbell Island, cattle from Enderby and Campbell Islands, goats from Auckland Island, and mice and rabbits from Enderby and Rose Islands. Planning for the eradication of Norway rats from Campbell

Sheep on Campbell Island
PETE MCCLELLAND

French blue rabbit
Pete McClelland

Island is under way. Eradication of mice from Antipodes and pigs from Auckland Island is feasible with current technology and is being considered.

Many introduced animals, particularly some rare agricultural breeds, are themselves valuable. Where the damage they do is incompatible with protecting nature reserve values it is imperative that their genetic value is protected by establishing a managed population elsewhere before eradication from the islands.

Key Visitor Sites

The following visitor sites have been identified by the Department of Conservation to enable tourists to gain an appreciation of the New Zealand subantarctic islands, without placing the most vulnerable areas at risk.

Bulbinella rossii fields
CHRIS RANCE

Enderby Island, Auckland Islands

Enderby Island (710 ha) enjoys sunnier, drier and somewhat milder weather than the rest of the Auckland Islands, and has been the focus of much human activity. It was utilised by sealers, European and Maori farmers (1842–56) and shipwrecked castaways. Many animals were introduced — pigs, sheep, cattle, goats and rabbits were released for both farming and as food for castaways. Some of these species have died

ENDERBY ISLAND

Map reference:
- △ Albatross
- ● Fingerposts
- ■ Basalt Columns

Features shown on map: Derry Castle Grave, Derry Castle Reef, Sward & Bulbinella, Clears, Stella Hut, Boatshed, Sandy Bay, Sea lion Rookery, Herb Moor, Rata Forest, Auckland Island Shags, North East Cape, Sward.

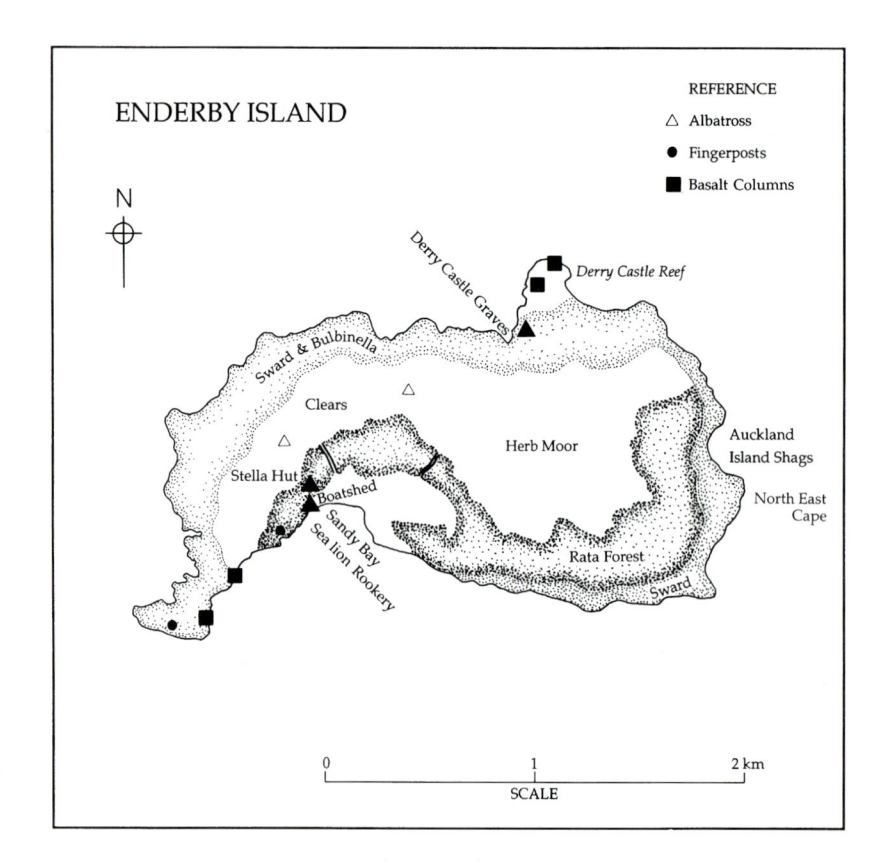

Scale: 0–2 km

out naturally and much of the island has been burnt over. The legacy of this human activity was a highly modified vegetation cover and populations of mice, rabbits and cattle. The cattle were removed in 1992, followed by the eradication of the rabbits and mice in 1993. The response in the natural vegetation following these eradications was immediate.

Although modified, the vegetation has its attractions for visitors. It is easy to travel through, and features *Bulbinella* meadows which provide a spectacular show of colour when flowering.

The lack of feral pigs and cats has meant several bird species that are scarce or absent on the main Auckland Islands are present on Enderby Island. The island also has one of only three major New Zealand sea lion rookeries in the world. Between 250 and 300 pairs of yellow-eyed penguins breed in greater densities here than anywhere else, and between 45 and 60 pairs of royal albatrosses nest on the island. Auckland Island shags and Auckland Island dotterels are also significant among the bird-life.

Two tracks from Sandy Bay provide access to the central herb moors. Travel across the moors is easy and routes lead past nesting royal albatross to Derry Castle Reef on the north coast. A coastal route around North East Cape can be taken to return to Sandy Bay. The overland return trip takes two hours and the coastal round trip four hours.

Attractions

- New Zealand sea lion breeding colony
- Southern royal albatross
- Rata forest
- Yellow-eyed penguins
- *Bulbinella* meadows
- Stella (Castaway) Hut (1880)
- Coastal basalt columns
- Auckland Island shags
- Auckland Island dotterels
- Auckland Island teal (flightless)
- Derry Castle shipwreck (1887) and grave
- Fingerposts (pointing to the castaway depot)
- Views of the west coast and main Auckland Island

Rata in bloom
Carol West

Erebus Cove, Auckland Islands

Erebus Cove, named by Captain James Ross during his 1840 visit, was the site of the British colonial settlement of Hardwicke (see History chapter).

The tourist landing site is in front of a castaway boatshed and derelict storeshed built in 1852, after Hardwicke's demise. Unfortunately the main castaway hut, which sheltered the survivors of the *Dundonald* (wrecked on Disappointment Island in 1907) was removed by the New Zealand government during the Second World War to prevent its use by the enemy. From behind the store shed a track leads to the Hardwicke cemetery, which contains the graves of settlers, their children, and shipwrecked sailors. The return trip takes half an hour.

There is no track along the coast through the former settlement, but visitors can trace the line of the old cobbled paths past the Victoria Tree to the *Amherst* Spar on Beacon Point.

Beyond Beacon Point is Davis Bay, the site of the Lieutenant-Governor's residence. Many of the house sites are still recognisable, particularly those littered with broken bottles, crockery and slates, souveniring of which is not permitted. A return trip takes one-and-a-half hours.

Alternatively, a route exists to Terror Cove (return trip one hour) by following the coast to the north.

Attractions

Rata and *Olearia* forests
Cemetery
Amherst spar
Davis Bay
Victoria Tree

German transit of Venus site, Terror Cove (1874)
Shoe Island prison (passed on approach to Erebus Cove)

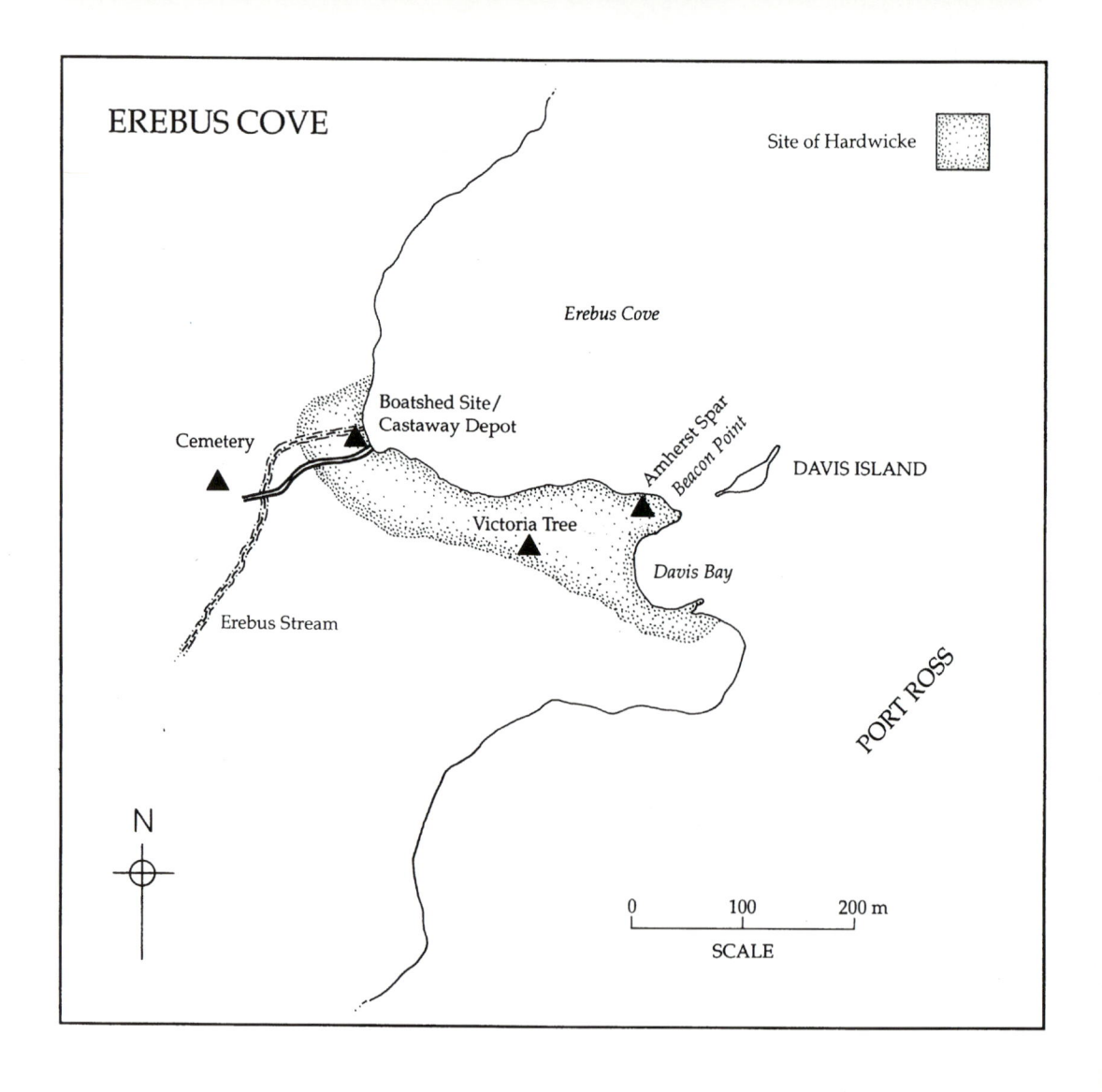

EREBUS COVE

Site of Hardwicke

Erebus Cove
Boatshed Site/Castaway Depot
Cemetery
Amherst Spar
Beacon Point
DAVIS ISLAND
Victoria Tree
Davis Bay
Erebus Stream
PORT ROSS

0 100 200 m
SCALE

Campbell Island

Until 1995 Campbell Island was the only New Zealand subantarctic island with people stationed on it all year round.

During the Second World War a coastwatchers' base was established behind Beeman Hill at Tucker Cove, which in peacetime became a meteorological station. The current station (Beeman Base) is on a different site. It was built in 1957 but closed in 1995 when all meteorological functions were automated. Only one building is now used for meteorological observations, although the Department of Conservation has its own base hut attached to the former accommodation building.

Campbell Island was farmed until the economic depression in 1931; cattle were exterminated in 1984 and sheep in 1990. The removal of the sheep has brought about a dramatic recovery in the vegetation, particularly the megaherbs.

The island is renowned for its five species of albatross, and is the world's most important breeding location for the southern royal albatross.

A track leads from the meteorological station to the Col-Lyall Saddle. Visitors can view nesting royal albatross, megaherb fields and views from the western cliffs. The return trip takes three to four hours.

Elephant seal
LOU SANSON

Attractions

Megaherbs
Royal albatross
Panoramic views from Col-Lyall Saddle
Meteorological station (access is not permitted to buildings)

Tucker Cove — farmhouse site, derelict coast-watchers' station
Sea lions — mostly immature bulls
Southernmost tree in New Zealand

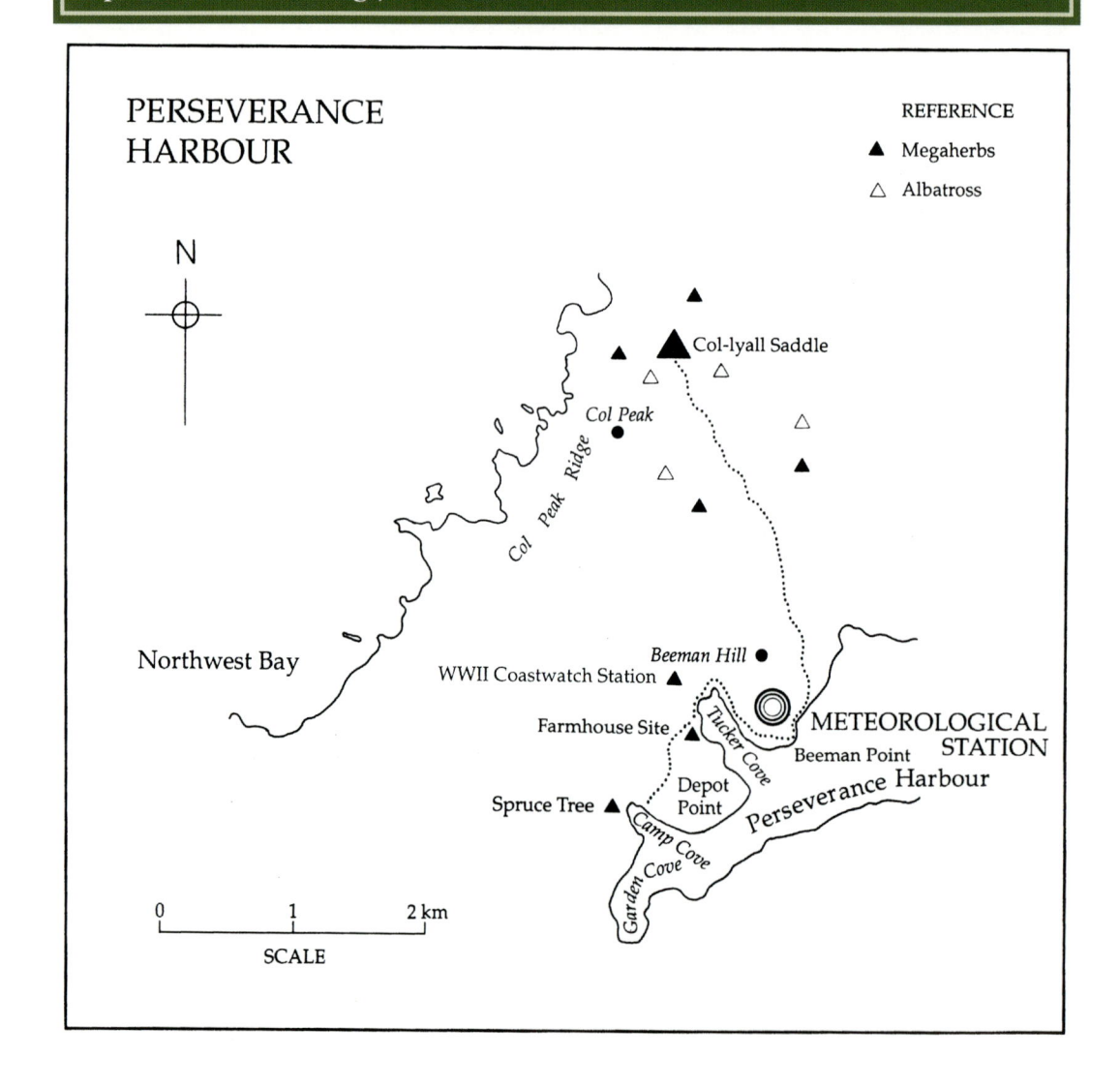

PERSEVERANCE HARBOUR

REFERENCE
▲ Megaherbs
△ Albatross

The Snares

Cruising the coastline in inflatable boats is the best way to get an appreciation of The Snares. One highlight is viewing the landing points of Snares crested penguins, particularly at Penguin Slope (see map on page 9). Tourist landings on any of the islands are not permitted.

The islands support an incredibly dense population of nesting seabirds. Their burrows honeycomb the island and simply walking on the ground would cause many burrows to collapse. The four endemic birds and many other species are also vulnerable to the accidental introduction of predators and weeds.

The dawn departure and dusk return of thousands of sooty shearwaters is one of the wonders of the natural world.

Attractions

Snares crested penguins
Sooty shearwaters
Coastal scenery
Cape pigeons
Buller's mollymawks
Western Chain islands

Snares crested penguin perched on *Olearia lyallii*
ANDRIS APSE

Code of Conduct

The following code has been developed to accommodate nature tourism in the New Zealand subantarctic, with minimum risk and disturbance to the environment. Visitors to the subantarctic islands should thoroughly study and follow these guidelines.

All the New Zealand subantarctic island groups are National Nature Reserves and entry is by permit only. Tourist visit entry permits are issued on the condition that the group is accompanied by a Department of Conservation representative. The representative's role is to oversee visitor activities and ensure there are no detrimental effects on the ecology of the islands.

Tourist landings are not permitted on the Antipodes Islands, Bounty Islands or The Snares, and unmodified or near-pristine islands in the Auckland and Campbell Island groups. These islands are free of rats, and the accidental introduction of these rodents would decimate insect and bird populations and cause extinctions. An appreciation of these islands can be gained by cruising off the coast in inflatable boats.

The Department of Conservation permits landing at designated sites on the following islands:
- within the Auckland Island group on the main island (Auckland Island) and Enderby Island only.
- within the Campbell Island group only on the main island (Campbell Island).

The Department of Conservation representative has the right to refuse entry to an island or change a landing site if there is a risk of disturbing breeding animals. Entry may also be altered or refused due to poor weather conditions or sensitivity of the environment.

Animal and plant quarantine procedures are strictly enforced to ensure there are no accidental introductions of new pests, plants or pathogens which could affect the unique fauna and flora of the islands. It is also necessary to be on guard against the spread of aliens between islands and within the islands of a group.
- All footwear and clothing must be thoroughly checked and cleaned before and following each separate island visit. No gear must be packed until immediately prior to landing, and must be sealed against rodent entry.
- No avian food products (chicken or eggs) are permitted ashore because of the risk of spreading disease to birds.
- No plants, animals or rocks should be deliberately disturbed or removed.
- No specimens or souvenirs are permitted

to be collected during tourist visits to islands. This includes historical material.
- No rubbish of any kind may be left on any island. Rubbish takes a long time to break down, attracts rodents and spoils the natural appearance of the site.
- The individual space of all wildlife must be respected at all times.

Visitors must:
- Give all animals the right of way. Wild animals, particularly seals, are extremely sensitive to movement and a person's height above the ground in relation to their size.
- Get no closer than 5 metres to any wildlife. Remember the subantarctic summer is the animal time for courting, mating, nesting and rearing young. Approaching too closely may cause parents to abandon young, leaving them vulnerable to predators.
- Do not touch any wildlife. Such action can jeopardise the bond between parent and offspring.
- Avoid surrounding any animal during viewing. It is important not to cause animals any stress or alter their natural behaviour.
- Keep noise to a minimum. Disturbance of nesting seabirds can lead to exposure of eggs to chilling, sunlight and predators.
- Keep to formed tracks and boardwalks where provided to minimise damage to fragile peat soils and plants.

Smoking is not permitted on the islands. Peat soils and dry vegetation during summer can create conditions of high fire risk. No toilets are provided at any visitor site.

Further information is available from:
Department of Conservation,
Southland Conservancy,
PO Box 743, Invercargill.
Phone (03) 214-4589

Further Reading

History

Allen, M.F., *Wake of the* Invercauld — *Shipwrecked in the Subantartic: a great-granddaughter's pilgrimage*. Exisle Publishing, Auckland.

Dingwall, P., 'The Changing Image of the Auckland Islands'. *Landscape 9*, Wellington, 1981.

Eden, A.W., *Islands of Despair*. Melrose, London, 1955.

Escott-Inman, H., *The Castaways of Disappointment Island*. Partridge, London, 1911.

Eunson, K., *The Wreck of the General Grant*. Reed, Wellington, 1971.

Hector, J., 'Notes on the Geology of the Outlying Islands of New Zealand'. *Transactions NZ Institute*, Vol. 2, 1870.

Kerr, I.S., *Campbell Island: A History*. Reed, Wellington, 1976.

McLaren, F., *The Auckland Islands: Their Eventful History*. Reed, Wellington, 1948.

McNab, R., *Murihiku*. Whitcombe and Tombs, Wellington, 1909.

Musgrave, T., *Castaway on the Auckland Islands*. Reed, Wellington, 1943.

Raynal, F.E., *Wrecked on a Reef*. Nelson, London, 1885.

Natural History
(includes geological references)

Bailey, Alfred M. and Sorensen, J.H., *Subantarctic Campbell Island*. Denver Museum of Natural History, 1962.

Bonner, W. Nigel, *Seals and Man*. University of Washington Press, 1982.

Camfield, Graham, *Campbell Island*. Curriculum Development Centre, Australia, 1987.

Clark, M.R. and Dingwall, P.R., *Conservation of Islands in the Southern Ocean*. IUCN, Cambridge University Press, United Kingdom, 1985 (reprinted 1990).

Cockayne, L., *Vegetation of New Zealand*. Verlag von Wilhelm Engelmann, Leipzig, 1928.

Cockayne, L., *New Zealand Plants and their Story*. Government Printer, Wellington, 1967.

Dawson, J., *Forest Vines to Snow Tussocks — The Story of New Zealand's Plants*. Victoria University Press, 1988.

Falla, R.A., Sibson, R.B. and Turbott, E.G., *Collins Guide to the Birds of New Zealand*. Collins, Auckland and London, 1978.

Fraser, C., *Beyond the Roaring Forties*. Government Printer, Wellington, 1986.

Harper, P.C. and Kinsky, F.C., *Southern Albatrosses and Petrels, An Identification Guide.* Victoria University Press, 1978.

Harrison and Brydon (eds), *Whales, Dolphins and Porpoises.* Golden Press, 1988.

Heather, B. and Robertson, H., *The Field Guide to the Birds of New Zealand.* Viking, 1996.

Infomap 260, Auckland Islands, 1:50,000 map. Department of Survey and Land Information, Edition 1, 1991.

Johnson, P.N. and Campbell, D. J., 'Vascular Plants of the Auckland Islands'. *New Zealand Journal of Botany* 13, 665–720.

King, Judith E., *Seals of the World.* British Museum of Natural History and Oxford University Press, 2nd ed., 1983.

Leatherwood, Stephen and Reeves, Randall R., *Sierra Club Handbook of Whales and Dolphins.* Sierra Club Books, San Francisco, 1983.

Marchant, S., Higgins, P.J., *Handbook of Australian and New Zealand Birds.* Oxford University Press, Melbourne.

Meurk, C.D. and Foggo, M.N., 'Vegetation Response to Nutrients, Climate and Animals in New Zealand's Subantarctic Islands, and General Management Implications, During, Werger and Willems (eds), in *Diversity and Pattern in Plant Communities.* SPB Academic Publishing, The Hague, Netherlands, 1988, pp. 47–57.

Meurk, C.D. and Given, D.R., Vegetation Map of Campbell Island, Scale 1:25,000 (1 sheet). DSIR Land Resources, Department of Scientific and Industrial Research, Christchurch, New Zealand.

Roberton, C.J.R., *Reader's Digest Complete Book of New Zealand Birds.* Reader's Digest, Sydney, 1985.

Sorensen, J.H., *Wild Life in the Subantarctic.* Whitcombe and Tombs, Christchurch, 1951.

Somewhat dated but still valuable accounts of The Snares and Campbell Island geology are in Cape Expedition reports:

Fleming, C.A., Reed, J.J., Harris, W.F., 'The geology of the Snares Islands. Part I: General geology; Part II: Petrology; Part III: Peat samples.' *Cape Expedition Series* Bulletin No.13, Department of Scientific and Industrial Research, Wellington. 1953.

Oliver, R.L., Finlay, H.J., Fleming, C.A., 'The geology of Campbell Island.' *Cape Expedition Series* Bulletin No. 3, Department of Scientific and Industrial Research, Wellington (includes a coloured geological map), 1950.

The sedimentary sequences of Campbell and Auckland Islands are described in two papers:

Hollis, C.J., Beu, A.G., Raine, J.I., Strong, C.P., Turnbull, I.M., Waghorn, D.B., Wilson, G.J., 'Integrated biostratigraphy of Cretaceous-Paleogene strata on Campbell Island, southwest Pacific.' Institute of Geological & Nuclear Sciences Science Report 97/25, 1997.

Ritchie, D.D. and Turnbull, I.M., 'Cenozoic sedimentary rocks at Carnley Harbour, Auckland Islands, Campbell Plateau.' *New Zealand Journal of Geology and Geophysics* 28: 23–41, 1985.

An excellent description of the glacial sediments and peat from Enderby Island, as well as a history of glaciation on the Auckland Islands, is in:

Fleming, C.A., Mildenhall, D.C., Moar, N.T., 'Quaternary sediments and plant microfossils from Enderby Island, Auckland Islands.' *Journal of the Royal Society of New Zealand* 6: 433–458, 1976.

The volcanic rocks of the subantarctic islands are described, analysed and summarised in several papers and reports:

Adams, C.J., 'Geology of the Antipodes and Bounty Islands, Southwest Pacific: Report of geological studies on the 1985 subantarctic cruise of HMNZS *Monowai* — northern leg to Antipodes and Bounty Islands 27 February–13 March 1985.' Institute of Geological & Nuclear Sciences Report 300, 1985.

Gamble, J.A. and Adams, C.J., 'Volcanic geology of Carnley Volcano, Auckland Islands.' *New Zealand Journal of Geology and Geophysics* 28: 43–54, 1985.

Gamble, J.A. and Morris, P.A., Adams, C.J. 'The geology, petrology and geochemistry of Cenozoic rocks from the Campbell Plateau and Chatham Rise,' in Smith, I.E.M. (ed.) *Late Cenozoic volcanism in New Zealand*. Royal Society of New Zealand Bulletin 23: 344–365, 1986.

The submarine geology of the Great South Basin, including the potential for oil and gas discoveries which would have significant impact on the subantarctic islands, has been summarised by:

Cook, R.A., Sutherland, R., Zhu, H. et al., *Cretaceous-Cenozoic geology and petroleum systems of the Great South Basin, New Zealand*. Institute of Geological & Nuclear Sciences Monograph 20, 1999.